the thing about Islam

the thing about Islam

exposing the myths, facts and controversies

Magsie Hamilton Little

First published in the United Kingdom in 2016
Published by Median, Max Press, London

10 9 8 7 6 5 4 3 2 1

ISBN: 978 1 906251 81 9

Printed by CPI UK, Chatham, Kent

Contents

Author's note

This book is not intended to be a pedantic guide to Islam covering every single aspect and detail of Islamic faith and culture. It would be impossible to offer a history of, say, Islamic art or politics within the confines of a chapter in one relatively small volume. My hope, therefore, has been rather to capture something of the spirit or essence of the many aspects of the Islam and the questions and issues that face it in the modern age, hopefully enabling the reader to gain a more informed understanding of the heart of Islam. Rather than a heavy academic study of the very complex subject of Islam, I hope this book is one that people might enjoy reading, becoming a more aware of the arguments and a little more knowledgeable. It has not been my aim to sit in judgement, but instead to try to offer a balanced, insight into Islam from an outsider's point of view, whilst avoiding the polemic, the biased and the sensationalist. I have tried to set out the facts, questions and issues as I have learnt, experienced, and understood them. Above all, my hope is that this work will set a platform for constructive debate. It is then up to you to draw your own conclusions.

Introduction

Islam is one of the three great faiths that rose from deserts of the Middle East. It began 1,400 years ago as a result of the experiences, teachings, and example of just one man. Like Judaism and Christianity, its influence has spread far beyond the lands of Arabia, and today there are over one and a half billion Muslims all over the world, spanning Asia to Africa and Australasia to Europe. It is the religion of choice for Inuits in the north and Aborigines in the south, and encompasses kings and prime ministers, shepherds and factory workers alike.

Islam in the twenty-first century is at the very heart of world affairs, including its conflicts, and its name is associated with some of the greatest terrorist acts of our age. Some argue it is an intolerant faith that condones violence. Others go even further, maintaining that terrorist attacks in recent times have showed Islam to have an inherently evil core. At the same time Muslims across the world have been left feeling that they have been subjected to hostility and victim-isation. They themselves insist that Islam is a peaceful and compassionate religion.

With such diverging opinions and heated debate, it is sometimes hard to know whom and what to believe. Myths, questions, and ambiguities have arisen over time, further confused by conflicting opinion both within and outside the Muslim world. What is the truth of it? What does Islam actually have to say about society, human rights, the role of women, marriage, and homosexuality? Exactly what is the real Islam? How can a religion that purports to be peaceful and compassionate ever be made an excuse for the human atrocities such as those we have seen in recent times in the bombings in London and New York? Similarly important questions arise from the mixing of Islamic and secular cultures. Should we adopt multi-culturalism? Or multi-racialism? Is the rift that exists between Muslim and non-Muslim something that can, in time, be made to heal? Or are just we too different? The current situation in the world seems a distant cry from the Prophet Muhammad's own call, under his famous treaty of Medina, for people of different faiths and races to work together to 'practise what is common between us'. What has gone wrong? Can we fix it? And how?

CHAPTER 1

The essence of Islam

In a religious life where faith, politics, and culture are arguably more inextricably linked than in any other religion, there are bound to be differences of opinion and controversial beliefs. Essential truths can be either vaguely known, interpreted variously, or just plain misunderstood. The Qur'an, the *hadiths* (that is, the sayings, acts, tacit approval or criticism ascribed to the Prophet Muhammad), and the *sunnah* (the portion of Islamic law based on his words and acts) are open to endless shades of interpretation, and can be twisted to justify different nuances of misinterpretation. This potential for mis-understanding was predicted in the Qur'an itself, which declares that some people will deliberately interpret certain verses in a skewed way. And sometimes, Muslims argue, the most controversial scriptures are simply mistranslated from their original Arabic.

The word Muslim literally means 'one who submits', but what does that signify? For non-Muslims the answer is often hazy. How can anyone sitting on the outside possibly understand the deeper meaning of the reality of a religion, if they have not personally lived it? Muslims themselves

1

often argue that the answer is personal, that the moment of realisation, or *ihsan*, when they are born anew into the faith, is beyond words. They talk about the many ways in which it is possible to be a Muslim, of *taqwa*, a constant awareness or consciousness of God, of everything they do or say being seen by him. There are, to a greater or lesser degree, many aspects of Islam – just like any other faith – that are by their nature elusive.

Although Islam can seem hard to define, most Muslims agree that at its heart it is strikingly simple and is based, above all, upon two ideas. First, it hinges upon the concept of oneness: there is one God and no God but the One; second, upon the concept referred to as *risalah* or prophecy – ie that God sends messengers, and that the Prophet Muhammad was his final Messenger, who was fortunate to receive genuine revelations from God. Gathered together into a book known as the Holy Qur'an, these words are as relevant today as they were when they were received 1,400 years ago. Thirdly, and almost equally important, is the concept of *akhirah*, of life after death: the earthly life is a series of lessons and tests, and the real life is yet to come. Around these three basic principles are five pillars of faith that underpin the life of every Muslim. They are oneness, prayer, charity, fasting, and pilgrimage. These are the fundamental cornerstones on which Islam is built.

The first step in any Muslim's path to worshipping God is the profession of faith: 'There is no God but Allah, and the Prophet Muhammad is his messenger.' This creed of Islam is known as the *shahada*, meaning 'I bear witness.' It is derived from the Arabic for 'testimony' or 'evidence', and acknowledges both God's oneness and the special role of Muhammad. The words constitute the first and most important of the five pillars of Islam: the five fundamental principles upon which the religion is based.

The *shahada* uses the word 'oneness' in its meaning of 'singleness'. The tenet that there is no God other than Allah is so important that it is inscribed on talismans that some Muslims carry on journeys to protect them from the hazards of the trip. The verse is also frequently inscribed on tombstones, so that the dead may have equal protection on their journey to the afterlife.

According to Muhammad's message, God's oneness is one of three basic facets of his divine self. The others are his transcendence and his omnipotence, each of which in some way restates his unity with the world. His unity is expressed in the Qur'an in one of its most famous verses, the *Surah Ikhlas*, which states that, 'He is God, One. God, eternal. He does not give birth, nor was He born. And there is none like unto Him.' No other gods exist beside Him: He is one in that He does not manifest Himself in different beings. This is similar in many ways to the creed of the Christian Church, and has the same significance to the followers of both religions.

The basic unity, or *tawhid*, of God, unlike the Christian conception in which the Divine is tripartite, composed of the Father, the Son, and the Holy Ghost, dictates that there is one God and no other divine forces. Nothing, in the Muslim mind, is like Allah. He is eternal, without beginning or end, outside space and time, and beyond human understanding. The great medieval Muslim scholar al-Ghazzali wrote that no one other than God Himself can ever completely know God, or should ever presume to understand Him and His works. Despite this, many names in the Qur'an, and in

3

common usage by Muslims, are used to refer to Allah. Perhaps the most common is *Rabb*, meaning 'Lord'. The Qur'an may refer more than 2,500 times to Allah as a name without modification, but in fact there are no fewer than 99 descriptions of Allah that are deemed acceptable. Among these are the Creator, the Protector, the Provider, the Mighty, the King, the Source of Peace, the Holy, and the Forgiver. Like Catholics, some Muslims find it helpful to use a kind of rosary when they are reciting the names that describe Allah and His attributes, but some very strict Muslims, such as the Wahhabis, disapprove of this custom.

Questioning Allah's *tawhid* is a very serious sin. Those who were surprised by the trouble caused by Salman Rushdie's book *The Satanic Verses* failed to understand that in questioning the singularity of God the book ignored, or subverted, the supreme importance that all Muslims bestow on God's unity – in addition to being disrespectful to the Prophet. Rushdie's sin was to give credence to a pre-Islamic belief that Allah had three daughters, each of whom held divine power. The Prophet Muhammad's teaching holds that God had neither wife nor children, and that this would have been incompatible with His role as the Creator and the Almighty. To believe that God is not alone is to commit *shirk*. *Shirk* implies that God is not omnipotent but shares His power. In strict Muslim societies, *shirk* is so serious that the only appropriate punishment is death. The West regarded the outcry over the *Verses* as an affront to freedom of speech. However, the important lesson to be learned from the Rushdie incident is that, to Muslims, the central tenets of Islam are so powerful that they can transcend all other considerations.

CHAPTER 2

A messenger is born

At the very heart of those tenets is the prophet of Islam – Muhammad – a man who for the one-and-a-half billion Muslims worldwide today is also the last and greatest of all the prophets. In the opinion of all Muslims, Muhammad was a unique and extraordinary person, laying down the foundations of a religion that has inspired a culture and civilisation that have shaped our modern world.

Muhammad is as central to Muslims as Jesus is to Christians. In Islam, however, the Prophet's status is very different from that of Christ in Christianity. According to Islam, Muhammad was not of God, and, unlike Jesus, he did not perform miracles. He was not divine, but a man. He was the intercessor, one who interceded on behalf of mankind with God. Muhammad is sometimes translated as 'praiseworthy', and Muhammad is also referred to in the Qur'an as Ahmad, meaning 'more praiseworthy'. He is the messenger of God; as such, his experiences, and the desire to serve God, motivate the emotions and actions of all Muslims, who make the distinction between man and message. They follow the man, but do not worship him.

5

Some might say that any great leader has the power to influence those who follow him, even when he is not present. Children playing in any school playground will always be conscious of the presence of the headmaster, even if he is tucked away in his office. Soldiers having a quick cigarette break will be expecting the troop sergeant to come round the corner at any minute. Like those of any figure in authority, Muhammad's advice, example, opinions, and instructions are uppermost in the minds and hearts of all Muslims. Yet he has never been seen as an overbearing headmaster, and the great respect that is accorded to him is based, not on fear and the threat of punishment, but on love and faith. Despite this, the religion he brought to the world is now associated with violence and intolerance. How can this have occurred? Who was Muhammad and what really was his legacy?

For non-Muslims, attempting to examine this question with a neutral eye can seem daunting since, just as denying the oneness of God is abhorrent to Muslims, any criticism of the Prophet Muhammad is regarded as unforgivable by them. At the extreme end of the spectrum, when Salman Rushdie depicted Muhammad as an imposter and a satanic figure in his book *The Satanic Verses,* such was the rage it caused that copies were burnt and the Ayatollah Khomeini declared a *fatwa* against him. In Denmark, cartoons of the Prophet depicted Muhammad wearing a turban incorporating a bomb. The cartoonist thus not only accused the Prophet of violence, but deeply offended against the Muslim prohibition against any representation of Muhammad. The Prophet Muhammad was not only being criticised, he was being mocked. This resulted in either actual or threatened

6

reprisals against the cartoonist, and the editors of any newspaper or magazine in which they were reproduced. Dutch politicians who objected were also targeted. Such events highlighted the conflict between the importance attached to freedom of speech by the West, and the values and beliefs held passionately by Muslims. They also underlined just how revered the Prophet Muhammad is in the eyes of all Muslims and how a grievous sin it is to regard him disrespectfully.

Although Muhammad's importance is key to Muslims, relatively little is known about him outside the Islamic world. The Qur'an itself mentions Muhammad by name on only four occasions, normally referring to him by epithets, such as 'messenger' or 'servant'. There are no images of Muhammad (just as there are of none of any of the prophets), out of a respect for the oneness of God. Fortunately, the written sources for his life are extensive. We are able to know a great deal about Muhammad from the *hadiths* (the sayings of Muhammad and other commentators) and the *sunnah* (the portion of Islamic law based on Muhammad's words and acts), both of which contain a wealth of description that portrays him in minute detail. We know that according to tradition he was regarded as 'the honest and truthful one', and that he gained a reputation for integrity.

Descriptions of his manner reveal someone who was always impeccably polite, and who invariably showed respect to his elders. He is reported in one *hadith* as having said, 'The dearest of you to me are those who have good manners; the most offensive to me are the most boring and the long-winded!' Psychiatrists now commonly hold that one's behaviour as an adult toward children and animals is a good measure of personality. Muhammad's manners were not only always exquisite, but he was invariably kind towards children and animals, and this is said to have reflected his love of people and of God's creatures. The ancient *hadiths* also describe his expressions. He was not a dour, unsmiling man, although he could be quiet when thoughtful. He laughed readily and heartily, with an open mouth as wide as that of a dolphin.

We also know a great deal about his personal characteristics, his looks, even about his taste in scents (his favourite was musk). According to tradition, there was nothing distinctive about his stature. He is normally described as a little above average height, neither tall nor short, neither fat nor thin, but he is known to have had broad shoulders, and strong arms and legs. He stood out as a result, not of his physique, but of his personality. If he had one distinctive physical feature it was his gait. He is said to have walked 'as if he was coming down a precipitous hill, and leant to compensate for this'. He had one other unusual physical quirk that would have attracted attention. When he spoke to someone, he didn't swivel his eyes towards them, nor even turn his neck in their direction, but turned his whole upper body.

His black hair, as was the custom at that time, was long and curly. His large eyes were dark, contrasting with his fair skin, and were often described as piercing. They were framed, like the eyes of many Arabs, by unusually long eyelashes. His mouth was large, and his teeth are described as being beautiful. Although in no way a vain man, he applied kohl and antimony to his eyelashes, as this was customary. As many Muslims still do today, he dyed his beard, although accounts vary as to its colour, and set an example to bearded men by taking meticulous care of it. It is said that he patiently combed it forty times on the front, and as many times again on its underside, a ritual which, it is said, increases a bearded man's vivacity, intelligence, and can calm him. Muhammad, it was said, recommended that the moustache should be trimmed, whereas the beard should be allowed to flow freely.

We are told that his clothes were, by and large, modest. One idiosyncrasy was his fondness for coloured linen clothes, a taste that could even be described as loud. But he did not care for silk, for he thought that it had the slippery feel of skin, and so completely clung to the body that it was invented so that women could go naked in clothes. Clothes as adornments were of no importance to him. If he was sent rich clothing, he would invariably give it away, and appear happily in his old clothes. Clothing, he thought, epitomised material things, and as such was of no consequence. It should be said that although Muhammad lived a fairly simple, even ascetic, life, Islam – in contrast with Christianity – does not exactly frown on material things. Possessions have their place in life, and Muslims are encouraged to enjoy the fruits of their labours.

All this we know about the physical characteristics and personal habits of the man, but to try to get to grips with the heart of his message it is necessary to understand his life and experience. At the time of the Prophet's birth some 1,400 years ago in 570 AD, Mecca was a settlement that, according to many scholars, straddled a caravan route, something akin to the railway town of Crewe in the nineteenth century, or the port of Dover in the twenty-first. Such scholars have traditionally maintained that Mecca was located at the crossroads of all the major trade routes in Arabia and that it was at least a stopping point on the incense route from south Arabia to Syria. Yet one scholar, Patricia Crone, has disputed this, arguing the town was somewhat off the beaten track and that, rather than trading in incense, spices and exotic, luxury goods, the inhabitants traded in much humbler fare such as leather and clothing. Beyond doubt is that the resident families of Mecca came from two tribes, the Khozaa and the Quraish. The Quraishis traced their origins back for generations to Ishmael, a son of Abraham. As in any bustling and transient society, old Mecca had similarities to a bootlegging town in the Mid-West. Inevitably, it was dominated by larger-than-life characters, and was home to Christians and Jews as well as pagans. It was an age of what Muslims call *jahaliah*, or ignorance. There were no organised religions. This was a polytheistic society in which each tribe across Arabia worshipped its own god.

There are as many miracles surrounding the birth of Muhammad as there are Christian legends surrounding that of Christ. According to tradition, shortly before his birth the Abyssinian army was on the point of conquering Mecca. As it approached the city, the story goes that the elephant leading the vanguard of the troops refused to go any further and bowed down towards the city, as if in reverence. The army halted, taking the behaviour of the elephant as a message from a higher source; and as a result Muslims believe that God delivered Mecca because of Muhammad's impending birth there.

Another legend associated with the Prophet's birth tells how when Muhammad was born, a light shone forth that illuminated the world. This incident is recounted in the Qur'an, which speaks of Muhammad as a shining lamp who lit the world from the moment of his birth. Another legend, the origins of which are less understood, maintains that one day two men came to the baby Muhammad, cut open his chest and took out his heart, removing a black spot within it before replacing it. The usual explanation for this is that the men who were allegedly the first cardiac surgeons were divine, not men, but the angels Gabriel and Michael. The black spot that they removed represented the human potential for sin, hence the Prophet Muhammad was without what we would call original sin.

Muhammad's immediate family was poor. His father had died unexpectedly while on a trading trip before his son was born, and his mother was penniless. When Muhammad was just a few months old, she handed him over into the care of a Bedouin tribe where he was looked after by a wet nurse, Halima. Here he began his life under the protection of his grandfather 'Abd al-Mutalib, who was the sheikh, or chieftain, of the clan. Life was harsh, a struggle for survival. Having already lost his father, Muhammad was to suffer a further grievous loss when his mother also died. He was just six years old. His grandfather continued to care for the orphan as if he were his own son, but two years later he too died. By the age of eight, Muhammad was completely orphaned, and this was to have a profound effect on his outlook and personality. It was his uncle, Abu Talib, a rich trader who had become the new sheik on the death of the Prophet's grandfather, who now took the child under his wing and raised him as his own. As a boy, Muhammad worked as a shepherd. Popular among those who knew him, he was given a nickname: *al Amin*, which means 'the trustworthy one'. One story tells how one day, while Muhammad was accompanying his uncle on a trading trip, the caravan in which he was travelling paused at Basra. A local Christian monk named Bahira saw a light above the caravan. Immediately he knew that this was a sign that a prophet had arrived. Glancing at Muhammad's back, Bahira saw between his shoulder blades the mark of prophesy, and knew Muhammad was the Prophet who had been promised in his sacred books.

As Muhammad grew up and went through adolescence into adult life, he became a merchant or agricultural salesman. Abu Talib brought the boy up to believe, as his grandfather had always done, that there was only one true God. From an early age, he was known as a decent man, and he became a leading light in the *Hilf al Fudul*, an order of chivalry that looked after the rights of the poor and the needy. The first time that Muhammad is known to have played a part in public life was on the occasion of an incident in the annual truce between the local feuding tribes, a feud known as the Sacrilegious War. It is said that a creditor of one of the Quraish took a monkey to the fair, seated himself in a prominent place and began shouting, 'Who will give me such another ape, and I will give him my claim on such a one?' He named his debtor as being one of the Quraish. At this point, a brave tribesman came up and cut off the animal's head. The row continued far into the night, and soon a pitched battle developed, although the extent to which Muhammad took part in this battle varies between accounts. Some scholars claim that he was charged with collecting the arrows falling within the Meccan camp, bringing them over to his uncle for re-use against the enemy. Others say that he himself participated in the shooting of these arrows.

Similarly under dispute by scholars is the claim by some that Muhammad's initial attempts to find a wife ended in failure when his uncle refused him his daughter's hand because of Muhammad's lowly social status. But all agree that at the age of 25, in about 595, Muhammad was hired by a business woman named Khadija to assist her in various business affairs. Khadija, daughter of Khuweilid, was forty years old, fifteen years Muhammad's senior, and had been married twice before. Khadija and Muhammad tied the knot, even though a match between so much older a woman and younger man was almost unheard of at that time. In due course, Khadija was to bear Muhammad at least six children, four daughters and two sons, although their two sons died in infancy, leaving the girls Zaynab, Ruqaiyyah, Umm Kulthum, and Fatima, who was the only one of this family to survive him.

Muhammad's marriage to Khadija brought about a considerable change in his circumstances. He moved to a storied house that overlooked the central square in Mecca. In business, he rose from being a salesman to being the leisured husband of a capitalist. His new status gave him access to all the important people in the district. It also allowed him time for prayer and meditation, as well as the opportunity to consider the town's affairs, and to worry about the decline in the importance of pilgrimage. He became a local leader, discussing solutions to the problems that affected the district at an informal parliament that met on the stony street corners. The iniquities of tribal life disturbed him. He was upset by the treatment of the poor, the weak, and downtrodden in society. He also pondered an even greater problem: how to devise means that would attract the whole world, or at least the whole of Arabia, to the *Ka'ba*, today the sacred shrine of Islam and at that time a shrine that claimed a very ancient history for the worship of God. In the years to come, Muhammad would walk alone thinking, and as he did so he would wave his hands as he mulled over his plans to restore the pilgrimage to its rightful place in society. At night, when at home with Khadija, he would confide in her that he was aiming to attract millions of Jews and Christians to the *Ka'ba*.

It was to be more than a decade before Muhammad ventured to share his hopes and ambitions with others, although during this time he kept silent when in public. Khadija alone knew and kept his secrets. When in Mecca, he would visit Jews to talk to them about their faith, and would also ask questions of Zaid, a short dark man with a depressed nose, who had become his friend. Zaid had been a slave among Christians, and he told Muhammad all that he remembered of the Christian doctrine. Muhammad understood the Jewish theology and its dialectic better. The Christian faith, so far as Zaid's confused recollections of it allowed it to be explained, also excited the Prophet. He was a troubled man, seeking some type of spiritual truth. Increasingly, sometimes for days at a time, he began to make retreats into the sterile, windy hills around the town, especially to a cave on Mount Hira about three miles from Mecca, in ever more fervent meditation.

CHAPTER 3

Out of the darkness

Muhammad was forty years old, and the year was 610, when he had the call from God to be a prophet. It was a message from God himself, not from the Christians, Jews, or Samaritans, a divine revelation that was to form the beginning of what would in time become none other than the Holy Book of Islam itself – the Qur'an. Accepting Muhammad's experience defines what it means to be a Muslim today.

According to tradition, Muhammad had been disenchanted, enraged even, with the local tradition of worshipping many gods. Almost all Muslims believe Muhammad was unable to read or write, hence he was pure, and free of influences. It is written that one night, now known as the *Laylat al-Qadr*, on one of the odd-numbered days during the last ten days of Ramadan (the month that later became the Islamic month of fasting), Muhammad was meditating and fell asleep, waking in terror as an angel with mighty powers appeared before him. The angel was Gabriel. Muhammad later likened the experience to the angel squeezing him as if his life was being taken. Gabriel told Muhammad that he was the messenger of God, and that he, Muhammad, would be the one to reveal God's book to His people. The angel showed Muhammad some words, and ordered him to recite them. 'Read,' came the voice. The voice returned again: 'Read.' The voice spoke for the third time: 'Read.' As Muhammad heard the divine message being given to him, this single moment became a defining one in his life. As Muhammad ran to Khadija to confide in her, there was no doubt in his mind. The seeker had found what he was looking for.

Yet this first blinding revelation was followed by a long silence. Days turned into weeks; weeks became months. Muhammad lived in silence, doubting and questioning his initial experience, before one day the revelations began again. As they continued, he began to understand: God had given him a message, and a duty to pass it on to those around him. With the exception of a couple of years when no revelations were received, he was to experience more and more of them, until his death twenty-three years later. It was a divine message that would later become known as Islam. The words came from God himself, and it was these sacred words that were to form the Qur'an, the holy book.

Muhammad initially confined the mission to his immediate circle. After Khadija accepted that God had appointed Muhammad as prophet, members of his family also became Muslims, recognising Muhammad as God's prophet in this world. Over the few years that followed, the believers remained a small group, quietly practising the new Muslim faith that 1,400 years later was to become a major world religion, with believers in every country and continent. After this time, it is writen that God ordered

Muhammad to publicly proclaim the message of Islam. Muhammad obeyed the instruction, and so the Islamic faith attracted more and more converts.

No one achieves office, temporal or spiritual, without engendering jealousy and ridicule. Jesus was no exception. As Muhammad began to pass on what he had been given, it was perhaps unsurprising that so many of the local Quraishi tribespeople began to regard him as a threat. Even Muhammad's own uncle, Abu Lahab, the tribal chief, opposed his nephew's preaching. In particular, the Quraish feared that Muhammad's insistence on a single deity rather than many gods would mean a loss of business opportunities and the chance to sell pilgrims and travellers food, water, supplies and accommodation.

Muhammad was now to experience opposition and mockery from many who disbelieved in the revelations. They thought he was mad, possibly possessed by demons, or suffering from epilepsy. Indeed, he certainly exhibited some physical signs and symptoms, such as sweating, and suffering from trance-like absences. Muhammad himself was even said to be upset about these. No revelation would be received without great effort. He would sweat and go pale. He described the experience as being like having his soul torn from his body. He also experienced visions, the nature of which would vary. Sometimes they would appear for no obvious reason, while he was going about his daily business. At other times, he would see things while lost in prayer. Sometimes the revelations could be specific, for example the need for a tax for the needy, or giving a moral code based on responsibility. In Mecca they were spiritual and inward-looking, whereas in Medina they were to become more practical in content, forming the essence of what was to be developed into Shari'ah law by Muslim jurists two centuries after Muhammad's death.

Things only became worse. Although Muhammad said he only came to pass on the message of God, the Meccan authorities became increasingly incensed. When offering him money to stop failed, they replaced gentle persuasion with violent persecution. Such was the anger generated by the success of Islam that Muslims were often in danger of their lives. Slaves and women who became Muslims were vilified. They were attacked and humiliated, not only verbally, but physically. In the face of such force, in 615 AD two large groups of Muslims left their homes and migrated to Abyssinia, where they took refuge with the Christian ruler there, the Negus. Negus, it is said, was so impressed with the teachings and way of life of the Muslims that he agreed to protect them.

Their exodus simply incensed the Quraish further. For three years the Muslims were banned from trading and refused access to Mecca. As the Quraish imposed even tougher sanctions on Muhammad and his followers, they came under immense pressure to give in. It was a very hard time for all Muslims, and many were reduced to penury. Despite this, even when faced with extreme provocation, it is said that Muhammad resisted violent confrontation, facing his opponents with stoical, non-violent resistance.

Things were to deteriorate still further for the Prophet, when in 619 his own domestic situation was overturned: first his wife of twenty-five years, Khadija, died, and this devastating blow was followed, just a few months later, by the death of his uncle, Abu Talib, his chief and mentor. Still determined to spread the Islamic word, he tried to make a fresh start in the town of Taif, but was turned away there also. Attacks against him increased, and by now Muhammad and his small band of followers lived almost in hiding. It is unsurprising that Muslims refer to this time in the Prophet's life as the 'year of sorrow'. He had reached his lowest point.

For a time, Muhammad struggled on as a single parent to support his family, before he married the young Aisha, daughter of his friend Abu Bakr. This was the first of a series of marriages he would enter into, all with women who had suffered the loss of their spouses through death or divorce. Although the accounts of exactly how many marriages Muhammad entered into vary (some say nine, others eleven, and others thirteen), what is clear is that he used marriage to strike alliances with other tribes and communities; at that time this practice was perfectly normal, as was polygamy.

Muhammad's marriage to the much younger Aisha is seen by many outside the Muslim world as his most controversial one. Some scholars argue that she was sixteen or seventeen years old, but others report that she was just six years old when the marriage was agreed, before it formally took place when she was nine. Muhammad was then fifty-three. Controversy also rages about the number of his wives, since Muhammad received further revelations that not only defined marriage, but decreed that in future any husband would be limited to four wives. Muhammad himself would remain exempt from this rule. The Prophet was allowed to keep all his existing wives, but he would not be permitted to take any more. It was an exception to the rule that some scholars argue was perfectly normal. Most, though, hold that Muhammad's marriages were political, that he was creating a new community and the easiest way to do this was to widen his social allegiances through the marriage link.

Yet even in Muhammad's lifetime, when he married Zainab, the divorced wife of his adopted son, some people reportedly thought it shocking. And later, when Aisha once went missing, Muhammad's enemies spread rumours of a scandal. It is impossible to know the truth of this. Muhammad subsequently received a revelation that instructed women to cover themselves, giving rise to a deep controversy that has waged ever since regarding the veiling of women. The veil, in time became a symbol of identity for Muslim women everywhere (see Chapter 16).

In 620, the same year as he married Aisha, Muhammad experienced the second most important night of his life, known as the *Laylat al-Miraj*, or Night of Ascent. It is said the Angel Gabriel came to him during the night, and seated Muhammad on a winged horse named Buraqh, who carried him to Jerusalem. Although Muslims disagree over whether the journey was a mystical vision, a dream, or a physical journey, what remains beyond doubt is the extraordinary significance of the experience, which became known as his Night Journey. It was a crucial episode that would transform Muhammad's life. Muslims see it as a confirmation that Islam is part of the Abrahamic tradition, and as symbolising an abandonment of the tribal spirit of the past. It made Jerusalem a sacred city for Islam, second only to Mecca; and it is why Jerusalem, now under Israeli control, and particularly its unique and magnificent

Dome of the Rock Mosque, matters so deeply as a holy shrine to Muslims throughout the world today.

Islamic tradition tells that once the angel Gabriel and Muhammad had arrived in Jerusalem, Buraqh was tethered by the wall on the ancient Jewish temple. Muhammad then ascended up through the seven heavens from the place where Abraham had almost sacrificed his son and on which the Jewish temple had once stood. The exact spot is marked today in the Dome of the Rock Mosque with a dip that Muslims say represents Muhammad's footprint as he took off. Ascending through each of the heavens, meeting different prophets, such as Adam, Moses, and Jesus, he was offered wine, water or milk. He chose milk, symbolic of the middle path.

Finally, before they reached the throne of God, Gabriel left Muhammad to go alone to God. As Muhammad stood before the Creator, veiled and thus concealed in light, God instructed Muhammad on the single most important part of life for all Muslims – the rules of daily prayers. During the journey back, Muhammad told Moses that God had ordered Muslims fifty prayers a day; Moses replied that the congregations would never manage it, so he should go back to God and ask His permission to reduce the number. Fortunately, God agreed to a reduction, but again and again Moses suggested that Muhammad should return and ask for further concessions. Eventually God gave His consent to just five prayers a day. At this point Muhammad told Moses that he was too embarrassed to ask God for any further reduction in prayer time. All was well: God told Muhammad that so long as Muslims said their prayers five times every day, they would be rewarded as if they were repeating the ritual fifty times daily. This experience set the standards of prayer for all Muslims, as well as awarding Muhammad comfort and strength – a reaffirmation that God had not deserted him.

It came just at the right moment. Unrest amongst the population of Arabia was increasing. Muhammad was still mocked and persecuted in Mecca. Although Islam was still no more than a small religious sect surviving in the midst of a generally hostile society, Muhammad's message had now spread beyond the region, and the growing hostility gave rise to various confrontations.

In the year 621, a group of men and women from the city of Medina (then known as Yathrib) met secretly with Muhammad outside Mecca, inviting him to move to their city, where he would be honoured as their leader and arbitrator. The following year another, this time bigger, delegation sought out Muhammad once again, and on this occasion they struck an agreement. It was a deal based not on tribal allegiance, but on something that went way beyond blood ties: on ideology and humanity. This was unheard of at that time. The invitation inevitably incensed the Quraish, who wanted Muhammad dead. A secret plot was hatched. It was decided that each clan would select one young man, and these men would form a gang to kill Muhammad.

Over the next few months Muhammad's followers secretly and gradually left the city. On the night that the murder was due to take place, Ali, his cousin, bravely slept in Muhammad's bed. The murderers waited to catch Muhammad, but were taken by surprise when it was cousin Ali who came out instead. Meanwhile, Muhammad had slipped out of Mecca with his friend Abu Bakr. The two fugitives took refuge in a cave outside the city, where it is said by some that God planted a tree to block its entrance and caused a spider to spin a web covering it. The men pursued Muhammad and Abu Bakr in vain, eventually giving up and returning to Mecca. Muhammad and Abu Bakr continued towards Medina. The year was 622 AD. Muhammad had suffered humiliation and persecution for ten years.

This flight from Mecca to Medina is referred to by Muslims as the *hijrah* – literally meaning a 'cutting off'. It marks a turning point in Muhammad's life, marking the beginning of the Islamic calendar, and a break with the tribal spirit of the age. When at last the Prophet made it to Medina, it is said that so many people rushed to offer him refuge that he was overwhelmed by their kindness, and left the choice to his camel. It chose a place where dates were spread out to dry, and this spot was immediately given to the Prophet to build his new home. In Muhammad's honour, the town of Yathrib took a new name, Madinat al-Nabi, the 'town of the Prophet' – which is now shortened to Medina. Medina was at that time a collection of different communities, religions, and tribes. Muhammad's new freedom allowed him to build his own mosque there, which functioned not only as a place of worship, but as a community centre, an office, and a focal point for all the townsfolk. A slave, Bilal became the first man to call the faithful to prayer.

CHAPTER 4

Politics, faith and war

Muhammad was by now not only a religious leader but a political one. He decided that an agreement was needed with all the tribes of the town to formalise his role. Such an agreement between Muslims, Jews, Christians and pagans would be based on respect and mutual responsibility. It would establish the rules of law and of being a citizen. This 'Magna Carta' of the Muslims was to become known as the constitution of Medina. It is the earliest known model of government in Islam, and was seminal in its recognising of different faiths coming together to form the same *ummah* or brotherhood. Sadly, no complete copies of the original agreement survive. Some historians even argue that there was no constitution, and that it was made up subsequently. Yet the spirit of it was clear. It was a message of plurality, of mutual, peaceful co-existence between different traditions and faiths, in one single community. This important treaty contradicts the ambitions of any radical Muslims who might be seeking to develop one single, global caliphate of Islam. It is all too often ignored, and many non-Muslims are not aware of it.

Although Muhammad was now recognised in Medina as a man of peace and reconciliation, his enemies in Mecca continued to plot against him. He now received a series of highly controversial revelations urging him to fight back, including one, for example, which suggests 'persecution is worse than slaughter.' It is these verses from the Qur'an that have given some modern Muslim groups, in particular Salafi jihadists, *carte blanche* to wage war against their enemies, in their own eyes granting permission to carry out violence. Moderate Muslims, however, refer back to life of the Prophet himself, arguing that *jihad* is not about nationalism, tyranny, or aggrandisement, but that it is acceptable only as a defence in the face of oppression.

With the Quraish opponents continually refusing to leave Muhammad in peace, the Prophet was obliged to take part in sporadic warfare. In March 624, confrontation between Muslim and Quraish culminated in a battle at a place named Badr. It was the first time the Muslims had gone to war in the name of God. Although Muhammad's followers were outnumbered by the Quraish, the Meccans were defeated. It was an extraordinary achievement. For the Muslims the victory was a vindication of their struggle over the past fourteen years - a symbol of their acceptance by God Himself. Muhammad now received a further, significant revelation that awarded the Muslims a new, unique identity. God now instructed him to change the direction in which Muslims performed their prayers. From now onwards they would pray not towards Jerusalem, but towards Mecca. It was a symbolic change, an act of defiance, and at the same time a move that made the relationship between Jews and Muslims very difficult.

A second battle at Uhud proved less auspicious for the Muslims than at Badr, ending in stalemate. The more powerful Muhammad became, the more his relationship with the Jews and some of the pagans deteriorated. The Prophet now faced a dual threat – from the outside and from within. By March 627, violence against the Muslims had reached a critical point. Abu Sufyan of the Quraish raised a massive army of 10,000 men and advanced on Medina, supported by the Qurayza, a Jewish tribe that had signed up to the Medina treaty, but which had secretly turned against the Prophet. In order to protect the city Muhammad ordered a great ditch to be dug. After a siege that lasted two weeks the opposition finally withdrew. The battle became known as the Battle of the Trench.

Defeat of such a massive, powerful army was a great triumph, but it was also one that was to present a moral dilemma for the Prophet. In the face of the betrayal they had suffered, Muhammad had to act, and at that time treason was punishable by death. He ordered his followers to surround the village of the Qurayza and appointed a local tribal leader to pass judgement. Shocked by their treachery, the leader quoted from Deuteronomy, 'When the Lord your God gives them over to you, and you defeat them, then you must utterly destroy them, and make no covenant with them and show mercy to them.' It was these words from the Bible that sealed the fate of the men who had betrayed Muhammad. They were all executed.

The act branded Muhammad as a bloodthirsty, brutal man. How could a Prophet of God conceivably order a massacre of some 800 men? Muslims argue it had nothing to do with the fact that the men were Jewish, had nothing to do with anti-Semitism: they say we have to see the event in the brutal context of the age. Indeed, as if to prove the point, shortly afterwards Muhammad married one of the Jewish widows, Rayhana bint Zayd. Yet some historians argue that the massacre at that time had an impact on the Islamic attitude towards Jews, and that some parts of Islam have taken the account and confused it in order to condemn Jewish people. Most Muslims condemn this interpretation as abhorrent racism.

The terrible slaughter at Qurayza was certainly in stark contrast to the very high moral example Muhammad continued to set according to the accounts of his lifetime, and his work doing good, and reforming society. He had become a powerful man, but by all accounts he lived modestly, giving much away in charity and as gifts. He comes across in the *hadiths* as warm and humane, and in many contexts as an extremely fair person, scrupulous about corruption, an exemplary human being, a great spiritual and political leader, and a searcher for truth.

By then in his late fifties, Muhammad now longed to return to the city of Mecca, the city where he had been born, and to make a pilgrimage to the holy shrine of the *Ka'ba*. In the year 628 he set off, with the support of around 1,400 men, who were unarmed, and dressed in the simple white pilgrim dress. Such a decision to venture without weapons or defences into enemy territory must have been astonishing. Muhammad had supporters in Mecca and their number was growing, but they were still in the minority. It is written that when the Prophet's party reached the gates, they were refused entry and turned back. Muhammad, undaunted, arranged that his men should make their sacrifices at Hudaybiyah, a village not far from Mecca, where he began a series of negotiations. While his supporters remained encamped at Hudaybiyah, they were visited by a delegation representing the Quraish tribe. Suhayl ibn Amr representing the Quraish and Muhammad negotiated a deal that they would keep the peace for ten years. The treaty came at a price: Muhammad would be able to return to Mecca the following year, but Sohail would not allow Muhammad to be acknowledged as the Prophet of God. Muhammad agreed, striking the words himself from the treaty in order to secure a peace between the parties.

In a society where honour was paramount, this act consituted an extraordinary offensive. Muhammad wanted peace. Thus the treaty of Hudaybiyah marked a milestone for him and everything he stood for. Crucially, he was prepared to suffer personal humiliation to achieve peace. The sacrifice was not in vain. Muhammad received a new revelation confirming that he had not been defeated, but that the treaty was a victory. In signing a deal of peace, he had extracted the crucial acknowledgement that he and the Quraish were equals. Through careful diplomacy, Muhammad had proved that peace was better than war.

It seems similarly extraordinary, in the light of this, that the terrorist groups of today can claim Muhammad as their inspiration, referring constantly to him to justify their actions and citing a revelation known today in the Qur'an as the *Ayat al-sayf*, the Ayah of the Sword or the Sword verse. The controversial revelation has been variously interpreted. The scholar Abdullah Yusuf Ali translates it as, 'But when the forbidden months are past, then fight and slay the Pagans wherever ye find them, and seize them, beleaguer them, and lie in wait for them in every stratagem (of war); but if they repent, and establish regular prayers and practise regular charity, then open the way for them: for Allah is Oft-forgiving, Most Merciful.'

Moderate Muslims argue that such revelations as this deal with a specific time in Muhammad's life when the Muslims were under attack and defending their position against the Quraish. They stress that there were no recorded instances of deliberate attacks by Muslims in Muhammad's lifetime, and that all the rules of engagement are spelt out in great detail, ensuring that women, children, the elderly, and priests are exempt from any violence. They argue that the basic concept of *jihad* has changed over time, particularly in the modern age.

Under the treaty of Hudabiyah, the pilgrimage to Mecca was repeated by Muhammad and his followers in 629, and this time the Muslims were allowed in, and hence into all the holy places, without opposition. The event marked a change in perception towards the Muslims, as people saw how respectful they were. Muhammad continued with his mission to spread the faith, sending letters to leaders of the surrounding lands, inviting them to consider Islam. From there, he hoped to extend the influence of Islam from Byzantium to Abyssinia. He was to be disappointed. Only the Abyssinians accepted *en masse*. But he gained support from many, especially Arabs who had previously followed Christianity. Following later aggression by non-Muslims, and another successful march on Mecca by Muhammad and his followers, he became established as the most powerful man in the city.

Sadly, the treaty of Hudaybiya did not hold, for in November 629 the Meccans attacked one of the tribes allied with the Muslims. With grounds for marching on Mecca, Muhammad now gathered together a huge army of 10,000 men and marched to outside the city. What he did next left everyone stunned. Instead of taking revenge, he gave an amnesty, declaring that no one should be forced to convert to Islam. He had come not to wage war, he said, but to restore the *Ka'ba* to rightfully honouring the one true God. He entered the city of Mecca triumphantly, went straight to the *Ka'ba* shrine and performed the ritual circumambulation seven times. He then entered the shrine and set about destroying the idols that defiled the *Ka'ba*, casting out all evidence of the other gods who were being worshipped at the time, wiping their images from the walls, removing their effigies and cleansing the rituals that had been debased. Those people from Mecca who had worshipped Hubal, the moon god, or al'Uzza, the mighty one, and had paid homage to other beliefs that were not far removed from the openly pagan, were stopped in their tracks. It was a bloodless conquest of Mecca, using peace and reconciliation, rather than violence. And it proved a winning strategy. Muhammad pardoned the Meccans, showering them with gifts and kindnesses, and returned home to Medina, triumphing through peace and integrity.

The Prophet did not live long to enjoy a peaceful rule. He returned to his home in Medina, but his army was obliged to conduct further war against tribes that attacked them, shocked by the desecration of their idols at Mecca. But events outside Arabia now worked to the advantage of Islam. The Western part of the Roman Empire was overrun by barbarians, and, in the east, the Byzantines in Constantinople had fallen into confusion through internal conflicts and inefficient rule. The Persian Sassanid empire had engaged the Byzantines in conflict for some thirty years, and had successfully attacked Jerusalem. By 630, the Byzantines had retaken Jerusalem, and the Persian influence was low, leaving a political vacuum for the warriors of Islam to occupy.

By 632, Muhammad had effectively become ruler of Arabia, having created a level of peace and security the people had rarely known. In March of that year he made his one complete Muslim *hajj* to the *Ka'ba*, outlining all the Muslim rites, known as the *hajjat al-wida*, or Final Pilgrimage. During this pilgrimage, the revelations about the rules of the *hajj* were given to him, and they are followed to this day. From this moment on, only Muslims were permitted within the city limits.

When the Prophet Muhammad arrived at Mount Arafat, he delivered what is known as his Final Sermon. It was a speech that was to set the agenda for the whole of Islamic society and sum up his mission. It is of such importance that it can be found in mosques all over the world to this day. At the end of it he quoted from one of his final revelations. 'Today I have perfected your religion for you, and I have completed My blessing upon you; and I have approved Islam as your religion.' He then went on to say that 'An Arab has no superiority over a non-Arab. A white has no superiority over a black, nor a black over a white, except by piety and good deeds. Every Muslim is a brother or sister to every other Muslim.' Muhammad's message was unequivocal: it is not only Muslims who are equal to each other; the equality relates to all human beings whatever their race.

As the Prophet returned home to Medina, he began making preparations for an expedition to the Syrian border, but he became ill and developed a heavy fever. He continued to attend and lead the prayers in the mosque as far as he was able, supported by Ali, but when too ill he requested Abu Bakr to take his place. He did not recover, and eventually collapsed. His wives realised that he wished to be with Aisha, and moved him into her room, where he died in her arms on 8 June 632. He was sixty-three years old. His last words were said to have been, 'I have chosen the most exalted companions, in Paradise.' His followers found it hard to believe their Prophet had died like a mortal man, but his friend Abu Bakr reminded them of the revelation after Uhud: 'Muhammad is but a messenger, and messengers have passed away before him. If he die, or is slain, will you then turn back?' He was buried in Aisha's room, which is now a holy shrine and part of the modern mosque complex at Medina.

In the light of all this, it is hard to believe Muhammad would have condoned the acts of violence committed today in the name of his religion. From what we know, the Prophet during his lifetime created a united and coherent society with human values. Arabia had become a better place than it had been before. When he took up arms, he did so in defence. And, above all, he preached tolerance and understanding, teaching that all of us are equal before God. Crucially, the Prophet Muhammad's ultimate victory was achieved by peaceful negotiation, but the responsibility to carry his message accurately now lay with others.

CHAPTER 5

Muhammad's legacy

Spreading the word of Islam was now a serious business. Within three years of Muhammad's death, Muslim armies had, in the name of Islam, won control of Arabia. They had also advanced into non-Muslim lands ruled by Byzantium and by the Sassanids. Five years later the Muslims had conquered Syria, Iraq, and Jerusalem, and in a decade they had added Egypt to their portfolio of triumph. Many of the early Muslims were primarily farmers or merchants trading in gold, skins, spices, textiles, and agricultural equipment. As business flourished, so the new religion of Islam spread along all the great ancient trading routes that ran from East Africa to India.

By 670 the whole of central Asia and northern Africa was in Muslim hands. Half a century later they had invaded Spain, Persia, and India. Muhammad's message had by now spread outwards to the east and to the west for a span of almost 6,000 miles. Muslim control extended over most of the Middle East, northern Africa, the Iberian Peninsula, and into France. It was not until the year 732 that the advance of the Muslim troops was finally halted near Poitiers by an army under the leadership of Charles Martel, an ancestor of the famous Charlemagne. The bonds of their faith gave the Muslim warriors a new strength, and a determination to spread the word. Contrary to popular belief, Muslims point out that no one was forced to convert to Islam at the point of the sword. The Qur'an stated clearly, 'Let there be no compulsion in religion.' Despite this, the Muslim invaders levied taxes against Christians and Jews who resisted conversion. Those who converted to Islam lived tax-free.

Within a hundred years of the Prophet's death, many aspects of his peaceful mission were being torn to shreds. Muhammad's successors argued amongst themselves, and deep schisms appeared which would lead eventually to the gulf between the Sunni and Shi'a, a rift that still divides the Muslim world. In the early days of the faith, those Muslims later to be known as Sunnis followed the teachings of Abu Bakr, the friend of Muhammad who become the first Caliph. Those who are now called Shi'as had wanted Ali ibn Abi Talib, the Prophet's cousin, to succeed him. The supporters of Abu Bakr accepted his succession as Caliph, but the Shi'as formed a breakaway movement. Shi'as insist that it was always the wish of the Prophet Muhammad that he should be succeeded by Ali, that he had marked out Ali as his successor and had made no secret that he wanted him to continue Muhammad's work for Allah. Sunnis said, and still maintain, that Abu Bakr was the best man for the job.

The expansion of Muslim power continued, despite many internal conflicts and divisions between Muslims. By the year 661 a great new empire had been born that was to continue and grow for almost half a millennium. Even so, it seldom managed to achieve either political unity or proper stability. Between the seventh and thirteenth centuries, the Ummayads wielded power from Damascus, in turn to be overthrown by the mighty Abbasids, who held court at Baghdad; ; and the Fatamids in north-west Africa and Egypt. Islam flourished under these great Muslim dynasties, though they faced fierce opposition – from Turks migrating out of Eurasia, to the Mongol armies of Genghis Khan and his successors from Asia. From 1095 to 1291, conflict with the Christian Crusaders brought war, political upheaval, and dynastic strife. From all this turmoil some thirty dynasties emerged, flourished, and sooner or later declined. Islam not only survived these great upheavals but became stronger. It assimilated the ways and customs of invading cultures, so that the later Muslim dynasties from the fourteenth and fifteenth centuries onwards (the Safavids in Persia, the Mughals in India, the Ottomans in Turkey, and the Mamluks in Egypt) were deeply influenced by them, and grew richer as a result.

This great ability to absorb the past, to change and to grow had been inherent in the teachings of Muhammad. Islam held that the universe was God's creation, and that in order to understand God it was necessary to investigate every aspect of his creation. Knowledge was essential in attaining the just and righteous life that forms the earthly part of someone's purpose, as proclaimed by the Prophet. The Qur'an laid great emphasis on the acquirement of knowledge by all human beings, irrespective of their age , background or sex. It attached great significance to knowledge, and it was this thirst that paved the way for the growth of society. Muslims received every form of inspiration for scientific and philosophical thought directly from the sayings of the Prophet and the holy scriptures, which invited believers to observe nature and reflect on it.

During the first few centuries after Muhammad's death, Muslim original human thought was adventurous and experimental. At this time, significant scientific, mathematical, and medical discoveries were to be rivalled only by those innovations borne of Renaissance Italy, the Age of Enlightenment or the Industrial Revolution. Drawing on the heritage of those such as Pythagoras, Socrates, Plato, Aristotle, the Stoics, and Epicurus, Islamic argument and discovery was heavily influenced by what is now known as Neo-Platonism. Learning was widely supported by even the most orthodox Muslim thinkers, even though, over time, an opposing trend gained strength.

Some religious authorities argued that the so-called dangers of knowledge for its own sake meant it could not be legitimate for Muslims. Knowledge, in their opinion, should be acquired only as a means of understanding God. Eventually legal and religious scholars attempted to define limits to the permissible scope of learning. Fortunately the cries of the purists did not prevent the extraordinary intellectual expansion of the Muslim world during the ninth, tenth, and eleventh centuries. Muslims sought answers to questions about the creation of the universe, the destiny of humanity, and about God himself.

In the centuries that followed, Muhammad's message continued to enlighten and enhance all aspects of society. Imperial patronage encouraged and facilitated Muslim achievement and excellence in art, science, mathematics, and literature, and by the sixteenth century Islam had extended as far as south-east Asia. In time the so-called golden age of Islam was eventually to decline. Still, the same emotions that drove the early followers of the Prophet continued to inspire the hearts and minds of the Islamic world in the centuries to come. Although the Empire of Islam had fallen, its message was very much alive, both in the teachings and sayings of its Prophet, but above all in the revelation of God's message laid down in the Holy Book of Islam, the Qur'an.

CHAPTER 6

The Holy Book

In the twenty-first century the Qur'an continues to be the unifying symbol of Islam. It is a metaphysical guide to the Islamic universe, the authority that determines Islamic law, and the fundamentals that determine theological teaching. The words of the *shahada* are the first that a father will whisper into the ear of his newborn child. From the moment it ushers the little Muslim into this world, the holy text will guide to the child for the rest of his or her life. Fourteen centuries on from Muhammad's lifetime, it forms a blueprint for living throughout the Muslim world, and its rules and prescriptions provide the pivotal moral compass for every Muslim. Its sacred power is unparalleled in the eyes of all Muslims because it is regarded by them as God's directly spoken word. As such it is unique among holy texts of the major world religions.

Such respect is afforded to the sacred book of Islam that copies of it must always be kept clean and in good condition. Nothing may be placed on top of a Qur'an, and it should lie facing Mecca. Before opening the Qur'an, Muslims should be ritually clean, or should at least have washed their hands. They will often have prepared themselves mentally and spiritually by contemplating Allah. They will normally sit on the floor in front of the Qur'an, which is often placed on a stand known as a *kursi*: it is considered disrespectful to let the book sit on the floor. It will often be kept in a separate room, or on a high shelf, so that nothing in the room is located above it. When it is not being used, it will be wrapped in a cloth to keep it from dust and dirt. Even the room containing a copy of the Qur'an will often be treated with reverence: Muslims will show respect in its presence, refraining from swearing or acting indecently. In their eyes it would be an unimaginable sin to defile it, burn it or destroy it as has occurred in the West in several incidences in recent years, resulting in riots and uproar – reactions that sometimes seem baffling and out of proportion to non-Muslims.

As the word of God, the power and influence of the Qur'an is so immense that it has affected not only society but language itself. Over the centuries, grammar and syntax have been developed in response to its unique, lyrical style. After the death of the Prophet, it was the study of the Qur'an that spread Arabic beyond the Arabian peninsula. In consequence Arabic influenced, or formed the basis of, many other languages, such as Persian, Turkish, Urdu and Indonesian. In order to determine the exact pronunciation of words in the holy text, the study of Arabic phonetics was pursued vigorously throughout the Islamic world. Artists wishing to perfect their transcriptions of the holy text created calligraphy, expressing their devotion to God by transcribing the words Muhammad had passed on.

The Qur'an is divided into 114 *surahs*, meaning 'steps up' or chapters, and further divided into 6,616 *ayas*, meaning 'signs'. These figures cannot be called authoritative, since there is no clear consensus among Muslims about the organisation of the Qur'an, and there never has been. For example, one modern version, based on the school of Kufa, gives 6,236 *ayas*. But we can make the general point that it runs to some 78,000 words – much shorter than the Bible. Estimates of the length of the Bible vary enormously, according to language and edition, but usually fall somewhere between 650,000 and 850,000 words.

The Qur'an begins with the *fatiha*, or 'opening', thought by Muslims to represent the heart of the Islamic faith. It is a summary of the message of God, and thus a mandatory part of the prayers that are repeated several times throughout the day. The *fatiha* is also read on other occasions, such as during prayers for the sick, or even to call on God's blessing for a completed business deal.

In the name of Allah, Most Gracious, Most Merciful:
Praise be to Allah, the Cherisher and Sustainer of the worlds.
Most Gracious, Most Merciful.
Master of the Day of Judgement.
Thee do we worship, and Thine aid we seek.
Show us the straight way;
The way of those on whom Thou has bestowed Thy Grace, those whose [portion] is not wrath, and who go not astray.

The *fatiha*, like its equivalent in Christianity, the Lord's Prayer, is divided into parts. It begins with an invocation that emphasises the compassion of God. It then proceeds through an affirmation, and concludes with a petition to God to give the person saying his prayers the strength to follow the path of a good Muslim and not be led astray. The *fatiha* perfectly illustrates the beauty of the Qur'anic language in its rhyme patterns and rhythmic quality. The *surahs* that follow are named after an episode or event of some kind. Some of them bear one of the many names of God – 'The Glorious', 'The Light', and so on. Some titles are more unusual, such as 'The Cow', which concerns divorce, the fair conduct of war, and the obligations of Islam.

There are many reasons for the largely oral tradition of Qur'anic retelling. Qur'an means 'recitation'. Importantly, Gabriel told Muhammad to recite, not to read or write. Since Muhammad was illiterate, he had to memorise the verses that came to him, and during Muhammad's lifetime the Qur'an was never actually written down in its entirety (although evidence remains that verses were jotted down on whatever there was to hand in the form of stones, dried palm leaves, pieces of pottery, animal skin, and even ribs and shoulder bones of sheep). Instead of scribes bearing the written word from one group of followers to another, Muhammad sent speakers to convey any new revelation orally, so the followers received it in just the same way as he had received it from God.

Only vellum, calf-skin parchment, existed in the early Islamic world. There was no paper. Books were the preserve of the rich, and it was customary to learn by heart. There were low levels of literacy, but the spoken word was intelligible to everyone. In addition, and perhaps more significantly, the Arabic script of the time was a *scripta defectiva*, or incomplete script. Many letters were indistinguishable from one another, and a great many variant readings were possible. Given that the Qur'an was considered the word of God, it was essential that ambiguity was entirely ruled out. Memorised oral versions were therefore considered preferable, and it became a priority to ensure the accuracy of the retelling. As Muhammad received the messages, it is said that he had to repeat them to the Angel Gabriel at every Ramadan, and that each was checked twice not long before Muhammad's death. The inability of anyone, therefore, to dispute the authenticity of the Qur'an gave rise to the concept of its inimitability, which is an essential belief in Islam. Many Muslims believe that when the Qur'an is recited, it is as if God Himself is speaking; just as Christians believe that Christ's presence, even his body, is with them when they take communion.

The Qur'an lends itself readily to vocalisation, being written in rhyming, rhythmic prose. The Qur'anic style of language – which is very different from the colloquial Arabic of its day – is not only regarded as holy, but also as beautiful by Muslims whose ears have been trained to hear it since they were born. When read aloud, its lyrical phrasings are full of music, making extensive use of assonance and alliteration. The number of syllables in each line varies, and there is no fixed metre, as one might expect in Latin verse. The verses are full of vivid visual imagery and this, together with the way that they are delivered, plays a crucial role in the appeal of the Qur'an to faithful followers – especially to those of us who do not fully understand what is being said.

As children at home with their families, and later, as adolescents, young Muslims will hear the Qur'an recited frequently throughout the day. They will learn from an early age, usually around seven, to recite and study the passages needed to perform the five daily prayers. Not only will Muslims hear the Qur'an, but they will see its verses displayed everywhere: from over shops and doorways to headwear and trinkets. Passages from it decorate the walls of mosques, and the arches that lead to public buildings, such as schools and hospitals. In some Muslim countries, in households where a family member is about to undertake a journey, the traveller will leave by walking under a copy of the Qur'an held aloft by another member of the family.

According to tradition, the Qur'an should be read with heart, soul, and mind. Although many Muslims do not understand the original Arabic in which it is written, all are taught the main passages of the Qur'an in its original language. Even reading the sounds, though they are not understood, is a privilege and an honour. Certain verses from the Qur'an are traditionally selected and written on paper, to be carried in special pendants. These offer good luck and protection against evil. In a practice frowned on by the orthodox who say it is wrong and may be of cultural ignorance, some Muslims copy parts of the Qur'an on to paper, then dissolve the ink off the paper and drink it. The ink is reputed to have great healing powers. If a Muslim goes to a Shari'ah court to give evidence, he will swear on the Qur'an that the evidence he gives is the truth, just as in a common law court most witnesses will swear on the Bible.

An ability to recite the Qur'an well remains one of the most highly regarded performing skills in Muslim countries. The art and expertise required are as critically and ardently discussed as Western opera buff would discuss the voices of lead soloists. To become acknowledged as a celebrated reciter of the Qur'an, to win competitions, and even to acquire a following, is not just a satisfaction of earthly ambitions: one who delivers the verses of the Qur'an movingly confers a blessing on both himself and the listener.

The solemn reading of the Qur'an is known as *tajweed* (what in the Jewish tradition would be called cantillation). *Tajweed* describes the musical reading of the holy word, and serves to emphasise its meanings. From the very beginnings of Islam, the musical rendition of the verses was considered an intrinsic part of worship: a remarkable science evolved that has established the art of recitation as a serious scholarly project. Rhythm and a melodic diction are recognised as positively enhancing the meaning and significance of Qur'anic verses, in an extraordinarily advanced form of rhetorical study. This art depends as much on carefully placed pauses as on the words themselves.

Once a person can memorise the entire Qur'an, which is not uncommon among the gifted or scholarly, they are accorded the honorary title of *hafiz*: one who preserves the Qu'ran in his heart. To recite it beautifully, in a way that draws out all the nuances of its language, ranks as highly in a Muslim's estimation as maybe a fine performance of Shakespeare would to a non-Muslim, but with all the added resonance and significance a religious text entails. It is not only those who recite the Qur'an elegantly who receive praise. So too do those who can write it beautifully. Calligraphy ranks with architecture as one of the two great artistic triumphs of traditional Islamic culture, owing to the limitations imposed upon Islamic visual arts by the proscription against depicting people and animals – it is considered most disrespectful to make an imperfect representation of God's perfect creations.

Originally two close friends of Muhammad – Abu Bakr, who had fled Mecca with him and remained loyal to him, and 'Umar, another close friend and follower, were responsible for collecting Muhammad's revelations in a written form. Within two years of Muhammad's death in 632, 'Umar who was later to become the second Caliph – urged Abu Bakr to collect the Qur'an together, fearing that those who had the knowledge and ability to recite it might die in battle, and that the word of God might be lost with them. Abu Bakr sent for Zayd ibn Thabit, who sought out any recitations that had already been jotted down, whether on stones, palm leaves, or on bones. He also travelled the country collecting those recitations that had been kept safe in the hearts of men. Zaid then presented the written pages to Abu Bakr. Abu Bakr passed this very first version of the Qur'an to Omar's daughter, Hafsa, who had been one of Muhammad's wives.

By the time the third Caliph, 'Uthman, came to power, there were at least four different versions of the Qur'an. The Caliph, fearing that the word of God was being distorted, ordered that all 'deviant' versions – those that did not accord with the copy in Hafsa's possession – should be burned. The precise word of Allah was thereby preserved, and could be handed on from one generation to the next.

Nothing in the approved version of the Qur'an was included that had not been written down in the presence of Muhammad and two other witnesses. No hearsay evidence was considered; nor were any verses that could not be authenticated.

The early written versions of the Qur'an contained little of the extraordinary artwork we are accustomed to seeing today. Ancient scribes did not think it appropriate to embellish the Holy Book with representations of living beings, not wishing to detract from the words and their meaning, yet it was believed that handwriting was an indicator of character, so the early calligraphers searched for styles of writing that would be worthy of the Qur'an's content. As Islam flourished in the Middle Ages, sultans in the courts of the Persian Empire commissioned exquisite, lavish editions of the Qur'an, decorated in gold leaf and beautiful colours. The two main styles of calligraphy used in the copying of the Qur'an, from as far back as the eighth century, are Kufic (from *Kufah*) and Nakhshi. Kufic is a heavier, more angular style, used for formal writing. It was originally used for stone or parchment, and is generally considered more difficult to read. Nashkhi is a more cursive script, more suited to pen and paper; it also resembles the printed style of most modern Qur'an editions, as it is considered easier to read.

Whatever style, undoubtedly it is the meaning of words that matters beyond any other consideration. Their power and divine significance to Muslims cannot be underestimated, and the controversy regarding individual instances of provocative and disrespectful behaviour towards the Qur'an must be understood with this in mind.

CHAPTER 7

A life of devotion

While the Qur'an has always acted as the basis of worship in Islam, the concept of living as a Muslim extends much further than the Holy Book itself. Being a devout Muslim requires more than simply attending prayers once a week. *Ibadah*, originally derived from the Arabic *abad*, literally meaning 'servant', is the commonly used term that sums up the way in which honouring and communicating with God is a constant state that involves all aspects of a Muslim's life.

Worshipping God is a concept often referred to by Muslims in terms of its five different component parts – *ihsan, iman, amal, jihad* and *din. Ihsan,* meaning 'realisation', relates to a conscious awareness of the Divine Presence, in conjunction with striving to connect with that Being. In simple Arabic it also means 'the pursuit of excellence'. *Iman,* or 'faith' is a Muslim's trust in Him. *Amal,* 'action', concerns obedience to the five pillars of faith, and focuses on the practicalities of everyday living. *Jihad*, a term that has become synonymous with terrorism, in this instance relates to the conquest of sin and imperfections in one's own nature. It is about mastering everything from greed or selfishness to smoking. *Din* is the combination of faith and life, the complete commitment to Islam. Only through respectful obedience to all five characteristics of worship can a Muslim truly put his or her faith into practice.

As in any faith, prayer is an essential part of worship. Muhammad set a template for his followers that not only consisted of living a life of modesty and piety, but of detailed rules of daily prayer given to him by God during his Night Journey. So long as Muslims said their prayers five times a day, they would be rewarded as if they were repeating the ritual fifty times daily. Then as now, prayer helps a Muslim to become more finely attuned to God, and provides a time in which he or she can escape everyday routine and earthly worries. It is a means both of purification and of spiritual growth. Through prayer, a Muslim connects with his or her fellow human beings. So much is it at the heart of a Muslim's life that the act of prayer is known as the second pillar of Islam.

Whereas in other faiths individual prayers, whether spontaneous or repeated, are encouraged, and are probably the rule rather than the exception, in Islamic ritual communal prayers are standard – required, in fact. These ritual prayers, and the ceremony that goes with them, are known as *salat*. Just as a service in the Church of England follows a prescribed pattern, and at various times in the liturgy the worshippers must stand, kneel, or sit, so the sequences of words in Muslim prayers are accompanied by different bodily positions. Adherence to *salat*, repeated five times daily, is so central to Islam that it is regarded by other cultures as being synonymous with the Muslim faith.

Many Muslims will stop whatever they are doing so as to pray at the five pre-ordained times of the day. This serves to remind Muslims of the importance of Allah in their lives. God comes first, and service to God is put above all other concerns. Prayer is not simply an expression of faith, but the means by which someone's personal faith is explored and enriched.

Some non-Muslims find this hard to understand. Some people might argue that nowadays it is difficult to find examples of true piety at all. We live in a secular society, in which there is little public worship. Charities are run like businesses, and the cynic can easily find psychological motives for altruism. But for a Muslim, piety – if not abnegation – must be a consideration in all his daily life, not just in the act of worship.

A Muslim must make every effort to be in tune with God, and aware of Him. This awareness of God, known as *taqwa*, is at the heart of the Islamic faith. The Prophet Muhammad is said to have defined it as 'worshipping God as if you can see Him, as He sees you even though you do not see Him'. This is part of the concept of worship as *ibadah* and echoes the concept of service to God taught by other world religions. And 'Islam', of course, means 'submission to the will of Allah'.

Such attention to prayer as part of daily life does, perhaps, not differ that much from the devotion of those Christians for whom piety is exemplified by the life of someone like Julian of Norwich or St Bernadette: pious Christians, denying themselves every luxury and ignoring their own wants and desires. Their food was plain, their living conditions austere to the point of discomfort, and they forswore the joys of sex. Theirs was a hard life, a frugal ideal that has found immortality in the many literary descriptions of monastic life.

Wherever there is a mosque, the call to prayer, known as the *adhan*, which consists, in part, of the words of the *shahada*, makes its presence felt. It performs the same function as a Sunday-morning church bell. Bell-ringing and the call to prayer from a minaret both take place at a set time before the service or prayers are due to start.

> *God is most Great*
> *I bear witness that there is no God but Allah*
> *I bear witness that Muhammad is the Prophet of Allah*
> *Come to prayer*
> *Come to success*
> *God is most Great*
> *There is no God but Allah*

In a Muslim city, especially in Saudi Arabia and in other stricter Islamic countries, shops and businesses close five times a day for prayers. Even in Turkey, generally viewed as more moderate, stereos in shops are muted at these times. Muslims have about fifteen minutes' warning before the prayers begin. The call of the muezzin is usually a live performance, but occasionally a recorded broadcast echoes from loudspeakers at the top of a minaret. The *adhan* is a universal call, echoing over rooftops and paying homage to the greatness of Allah. Unlike, for example, trumpet calls in a cavalry barracks, it does not usually vary according to the time of the day. However, in Sunni and Shi'i Islam the actual call to prayer does vary, and in both the *fajr* or early-morning prayer contains the additional line, 'Prayer is better than sleep,'. Likewise, the number of times the prayers are repeated also may vary, and may be at different times of day.

The first *adhan* is usually followed by a reminder call just before the commencement of proceedings known as the *iqamah*. Muslims can and do pray alone but most prefer to pray together. The first prayer meeting is early in the morning, before dawn, and is known as *fajr*; the second is at noon (*zohr*); the third during the afternoon (*asr*); then at sunset (*maghrib*); and finally at night (*isha*). The exact time of these varies from country to country. The timings, although they reflect the progress of the sun, change according to place and season, and timetables are normally provided by the mosque to tell people when prayer times begin and end.

Just as Sunday mornings provide an opportunity for worshippers to congregate in the Christian church, in Islam Friday prayers at midday, known as *salat al-Juma*, are the focus of the week in prayer. In Islamic countries, shops and businesses come to a halt, allowing people to attend, as laid down in the Qur'an: 'O believers, when proclamation is made for prayer on the Day of Congregation, hasten to God's remembrance and leave business aside.' On a Friday in Muslim cities, the entire community gathers in the local central mosque for noon *salat*, rather than attending the smaller neighbourhood mosques that have been used throughout the rest of the week for their prayers. Some so-called 'lax' Muslims, or those for whom work presents an impediment to frequent daily worship, attend prayers only on Fridays.

The meaning of *salat* is 'get together', the same term that is or was used in a thousand and one British villages and towns when 'a get-together' was a meeting of some family or group. Men normally opt to pray together, and in many Islamic cultures women pray together at home, or in their own section of the mosque. Almost every mosque in Saudi Arabia has a women's section, and these are usually full. If it is not possible to pray at a mosque, *salat* can be performed anywhere. It is better to pray in some unsuitable spot than not to pray at all. In a Muslim country, everyone at the appropriate time, and having been suitably warned by the *adhan*, will stop whatever it is they are doing, face Mecca, take off their shoes, and pray. If they are not in a mosque, they may spread out a prayer rug to kneel on, or even, if one is not available, a newspaper. Prayer rugs come in a range of colours, decorated with abstract patterns (since humans or living idols must not be shown) or even the *Ka'ba* or the mosque at Medina.

The pious are not restricted to the prescribed five prayers a day, and are free to perform additional ones. Private prayers, known as *du'a*, meaning 'supplications', may be said at any time. During the great festivals of the Muslim faith, the *hajj* pilgrimage to Mecca, and on other special occasions, even less devout Muslims will increase the time spent on their devotions.

The initial stage of prayer, before the act of praying even begins, is widely known as *niyyah*, which means the 'intention to pray': ie, a mental, spiritual and physical preparation, and a declaration of honourable intentions for prayer. The aim of purity is to be in a fit condition to face God. A man or woman who is impure in body or mind, or even by contact with that which is impure, is in danger of distancing him or herself from God. If impure, a Muslim is no longer allowed to pray, to recite the Qur'an, to touch the sacred book, or even to enter a mosque.

The purification or *taharah* is the process of cleansing that rids a Muslim of sin and impurity. Islam teaches the ways of remaining pure for as long as possible, and of expunging any form of impurity as soon as a person becomes aware of it. Purifying rituals are designed to remove anything that may pollute, whether the pollution is physical, psychological, or spiritual. This is no easy task, when daily bodily functions are inevitably polluting, and the mind too is often polluted by its fantasies. The Muslim who seeks purity in every aspect of life is as zealous, even obsessive, as the proud housewife who strives – but fails – to prevent the dust blowing through the window and settling around the house.

Washing, so as to restore purity to the body, is an essential component to continuing acceptance by God. It has also had the important role of protecting the health and body against the diseases that may easily spread in the prevailing climate if there is a lack of hygiene. Restoring purity as soon as possible after contamination by contact with either major or minor impurities is always essential. It is widely known that of utmost importance is washing before prayer, as was revealed to the Prophet Muhammad. This is known as *wudu* or *wuzu*. *Wudu* is a complex procedure that does not only wash away dirt. Muslims feel that when they pray, they have to face God: their washing ritual has to ensure that the purification cleanses mind as well as body. The Qur'an states: 'O you who believe! When you rise up for prayer, wash your faces and your hands as far as the elbows, and wipe your heads and wash your feet to the ankles; and if you are under an obligation to perform a bath, then go through the complete wash; and if you are sick, or on a journey, or come from the lavatory, or have been intimate with a woman, and you cannot find water, then take clean earth and wipe your faces and your hands with it. Allah does not wish to put you into difficulties, but He wishes to purify you that He may complete His favour on you.'

Muhammad taught specific and detailed rules about the act of cleansing. When washing, a Muslim should 'wash your hands up to the wrists three times; rinse your mouth with water thrown into your mouth with the right hand; sniff the water into the nostrils and blow it out three times; wash the entire face, including the forehead, three times; wipe the top of the head once with the inner surface of both hands held together; wash your ears with your forefingers and wipe the back of the ears with your thumbs and wipe the back of your neck once; wash the right foot and then the left foot up to the ankle three times; let the water run from your hands up to your elbows three times.'

The ritual of *wudu* doesn't have to be repeated before each set of prayers if a Muslim has remained 'in *wudu*'. Someone comes out of *wudu* if they have passed urine, faeces, or wind, or have had any other bodily emission of fluid, such as blood or semen, since the ritual wash. Anyone who has slept since the last *wudu* automatically comes out of it, and is required to repeat the wash. Muslims consider it is impossible for women to be in *wudu* if they are menstruating or still have a discharge following childbirth; and during this time they have a dispensation to be absent from prayers. After intercourse, or when they have completed menstruation, a Muslim doesn't only need a good wash, as provided by *wudu*, but a proper bath, known as *ghusl*.

Muslims are expected always to approach *wudu* as if it is part of the prayer, and to adopt an appropriately quiet and respectful demeanour. Even as they wash, they will often recite a prayer known as the *kalma*. When *wudu* is needed before prayers, it can be performed in a courtyard, inside a house, or even in the open desert – as may happen if on pilgrimage to Mecca.

Upon entering the mosque, a believer removes his or shoes as a gesture of piety and respect, and performs two sequences of prayers and bowings known as *rak'as*. Every Muslim, male or female, is required to wear clean clothes, and all are to be modestly covered. This sometimes includes covering the head, for which many men sport skullcaps. For women, it means the whole body, except for face, hands and feet. No make-up, nail varnish or perfume should be worn, although henna is permitted. *Tasbih* or *subhah* are beads that signify the ninety-nine known names of Allah, divided into three sections with larger beads. They are passed through the hands, during which time a Muslim prays with the words *subhan Allah* ('Glory to God'), *alhamdu l'Illah* ('Thanks be to Allah'), or *allahu akbar* ('God is Most Great').

Muslims regard the relationship between man and God as one to one, with no involvement from another human being as intermediary. Muslims, therefore, make a clear distinction between a priest and an *imam*, or prayer leader, who both leads the prayer and in many instances acts as the spiritual leader for the community. They hold that an *imam* is a person who has volunteered to lead, who is attuned to Islam, and knows the Qur'an well enough to recite it during the prayers. Although most mosques have an *imam*, it is actually not compulsory, and any Muslim can lead prayers. When the congregation is mixed, this person is a man or a boy, and he stands in front of the lines of Muslim worshippers. If women only are present, a woman can lead from the middle of the row.

At Friday prayers before the prayer meeting starts, it is usual for the *imam* or another learned individual to climb into the pulpit and deliver a sermon. This is based upon a text drawn from Qur'an and is preceded by a set form of words: 'O you who believe, when the call is proclaimed to prayer on the day of assembly, hasten to remember God, and cease your business. This is best for you if you understand. And when the prayer service is finished, scatter over the land and seek the bounty of God and remember God often so you may prosper.' In many Muslim states, the sermon often includes a blessing upon the president or chief of state.

All Muslims today pray in the direction of Mecca, just as was taught by Muhammad 1,400 years ago when he received the instruction from God telling him to change the direction of prayer from Jerusalem, which had meant turning their backs on their ancient holy site of the *Ka'ba*. This is known in Arabic as *qiblah*, which means literally 'to turn one's heart towards the direction of God'. The image of Muslims lining up in rows to pray, with one person in front of the main group, is universally known. Just as in a Christian church it is bad manners to turn one's back on the altar, in a mosque it is considered bad form to pass in front of someone at prayer. It is standard, therefore, for the praying area to be marked with a barrier, which originates from the Prophet Muhammad's custom of placing his staff in front and to the right of him.

The prayer ritual usually consists of two to four cycles of prayers accompanied by the appropriate bowings to God. In the course of prayers, the worshipper completes these words and movements, known as *rak'a*s. A *rak'a* consists of eight stages of worship, and the number of *rak'a*s required at different prayer times increases during the day: the early-morning prayer requires two; noon and afternoon have four; early evening three; and the night-time prayer requires four. After *niyyah*, or preparation, comes *takbir*, meaning 'glorifying', during which the outside world is forgotten. All Muslims stand, raise their hands to their shoulders and announce *allahu akbar* ('God is Most High'). Then, putting their right hand over their left on their chest, they say, 'Glory and Praise be to You, O God; blessed is Your name and exalted is Your majesty. There is no God but You. I come, seeking shelter from Satan, the rejected.' Next the *fatiha*, the most sacred opening verse of the Qur'an is recited.

After another reading from the Qur'an selected by the *imam*, there is a series of bowings known as *ruku*, intended to show respect to Allah. During these *ruku*s, Muslim men bow deeply, usually with a straight back. To preserve their modesty, women bow less severely. All then stand to acknowledge God, and say the words, 'God always hears those who praise Him. O God, all praise be to You, O God greater than all else.' After this is the *sujud*, or *sajda*, when a Muslim kneels on the ground in complete submission to God, touching forehead and palms on the floor. Their fingers face Mecca and elbows are off the ground. Then each person says three times: 'Glory be to my Lord, the Most High. God is greater than all else.' They then kneel up in a sitting position, praying silently for a few moments, before repeating the whole motion of bowing down once again.

At the end of the set prayer ritual, there is frequently time for personal prayers and prayers for others, and for the forgiveness of sins, a prayer that is often accompanied by placing right hand on right knee and extending a forefinger. It is not uncommon to see Muslims sighing and wiping their faces at this point. Finally there is the 'peace', or the *salaam*: *Asalaam aleikum wa rahmatullah*, or 'Peace be with you, and the mercy of Allah.' This ritual is almost identical to the 'Peace be with you,' spoken by a priest in the Christian church service; but in Islam it is directed not only at fellow members of the congregation, but at the guardian angels also present. At the close of prayers, many Muslims like to perform an additional voluntary two *rak'a*s, according to the acts of the Prophet as described in the *sunnah*.

CHAPTER 8

A place of prostration

Although the practice of worship is fundamental to Islamic daily life, the actual place of prayer has always been of less importance, whereas in Christianity and Judaism the architecture of the church or synagogue has arguably more significance. In Islam, so long as it is clean physically and spiritually, any building can be used as a mosque. Muslims sometimes refer to mosques as *masjid*, which simply means in Arabic 'a place of prostration or lying down': that which might be described as the Muslim prayer position. Often a simple prayer mat (or even a piece of wooden board) will suffice, so long as it faces Mecca. A tap nearby for the ablutions is desirable, since it is essential for a Muslim to wash before prayer.

Muhammad's original mosque was not a grand place of worship, but a simple building at Medina made with palm trunks, where the Prophet's camel came to rest. Here Muhammad marked out a simple fifty-metre square *dar*, or courtyard, framed by mud walls. Around the walls, there were huts roofed with palm leaves where his wives lived. In the centre of the courtyard, Muhammad dug a well.

When his companions asked that they should have shelter from the sun, Muhammad used palm leaves to provide it. From the earliest days of Islam, prayers could be held anywhere, since there were no customs that determined the formal architectural pattern of the mosque building. The pattern of building evolved later from the Prophet's first plan.

The Prophet's wish that a place of worship should also be a meeting place for the community is as relevant today as it was in his lifetime. Today a mosque provides a focal point for people, hosting youth clubs, and kindergarten, and child-minding facilities for younger Muslims. Somewhat akin to a village hall, rooms in a mosque can be hired out for weddings, birthdays, and social or family events. It is some time since churches have been considered centres of learning, but mosques still are. In addition to their other functions, they act as classrooms and adult education centres. Adults and children alike may attend classes to study the Qur'an and learn Arabic, with much of the teaching done by volunteers. There are normally enough volunteers to provide classes every day of the week. This is not so much the case in Muslim countries, where the Islamic community have greater resources at their disposal, and mosques can be reserved for prayer.

Muhammad's original mosque served as a prototype for all subsequent mosques, great and small. Its form and layout created a legacy for the future for all Islamic buildings, including initially those built under royal patronage; and from the eighth century onwards it has been the inspiration for all mosques throughout the world. Consequently, any building specifically erected as a mosque shares certain architectural and stylistic features, including arches and intricate geometric patterns; and, as with any architectural style, these features and their precise appearance vary according to region and period. The Great Mosque in Damascus shares the same courtyard layout as Muhammad's mosque in Medina. It incorporates the minaret, a feature that to the rest of the world encapsulates Islamic architecture. Clusters of minarets punctuate the skyline of every Islamic city, and the call to prayer that issues from them reminds everyone of the presence of both the mosque and Allah. Similarly, the design of the mosque at Damascus, like all great mosques, is based on the same principles, resulting in an identical formal layout. In particular, all mosques are correctly orientated so that any Muslim when praying can be certain that he or she is facing towards the *Ka'ba* in Mecca, as Muhammad instructed. All the great early mosques of Damascus, Cordoba and al-Aqsa were designed on the Roman basillica pattern.

The arch has remained a constant feature of Islamic mosque architecture. At the great mosque of Cordoba, the superimposed arches, such as were used by the Romans in ancient times for their Iberian aqueducts, are not just structural but a key aspect of the decoration. They are both functional and aesthetically pleasing. The same use of the arch spread throughout Europe and remained part of church architectural structure until the twentieth century.

Of particular importance is the *mihrab*, an alcove sometimes referred to as the 'niche of lights'. It is a symbol of the presence of Allah in the mosque, and so focuses the minds of worshippers towards God. The *mihrab* lies in the prayer niche on the main axis of the mosque, and is on the wall facing Mecca. This is known as the *qiblah* wall. It has a similar significance to the chancel and altar in a Christian church. To the right of the *mihrab* is the *minbar*, the place from which the *imam* delivers his sermon and which serves the same purpose as a pulpit. As with a pulpit, the *minbar* can either consist of a few steps leading to a platform, or, as in an important Christian church, it can be reached by means of a more elaborate stairway.

The *mihrab* and area around it is the most decorated part of most mosque interiors. The decoration will vary from country to country, according to culture and time, so that those in Morocco differ from those in Tunisia. The interior of many ordinary mosques may appear, to non-Muslims, sparsely decorated and furnished, with no chairs or pews. Everyone prays on the floor in the prayer hall, often on a carpet that is marked with lines showing where to stand and kneel, or delineated with prayer-mat-shaped squares – such as in the mosque in Regent's Park, London.

Decoration in any mosque is very different to that of Christian churches where images of Christ, the Virgin Mary, and saints vary according to denomination. Initially, all art in the West was church art: broadly speaking, it was only after the Reformation that secular art became acceptable. After the Reformation, Catholic churches remained highly decorated, whereas those in some parts of Scotland, for example, were totally bare. The perfection of God's creation is depicted in Islam an abstract manner, by strict geometrical designs. Representation of either humans or animals, although not actually proscribed in the Qur'an, is not permitted in any form in the decoration of a mosque, in order to prevent idolatry (*shirk*). Such representation would be imperfect, and thus disrespectful copies of Allah's perfect creations.

That said, mosques were often more colourful in the past than they appear today. Woodwork, stucco and marble were painted with red, lapis lazuli and green, and often with an abundance of gold. Coloured glass was also added. Ornament could also be used to frame accesses and openings within the mosque, but any exterior decoration was rare. Lavish detail and ornamentation was normally confined to the interior of the mosque, and helped reflect the importance that Islam accords to privacy. On the outside, what decoration there is is designed to accentuate the architectural outlines and the building. As ever with Islamic buildings, the glory is always within, and inscriptions from the Qur'an are the primary means by which architects and artists display their creativity in honour of God. These are painted or carved in horizontal bands around the building, highlighting and framing any architectural openings. The horizontal inscriptions often balance the arches and panels in a mosque interior. Geometric patterns are applied as decoration to the walls and ceilings. Palm trees and springs are often included, to recall the Paradise described in the Qur'an – as can be seen in the green and gold of the beautiful mosaics in the Great Mosque of Damascus. Many mosques also feature chandeliers, stained glass, intricate tiling, and lavishly woven carpets.

The number of mosques in Britain and in Europe has risen fast over the past twenty or thirty years. During the past century, church towers and spires presided over the skyline of almost every European town and city. In an average-sized town there was said to be a church for every week of the year. Each day, their bells summoned the faithful to worship, and on Sundays they rang for the three main services of the day. Nowadays minarets are as prominent as church towers and spires in many of the same cities, and the call to prayer from the mosque can be heard five times a day. It is not surprising that non-Muslims sometimes feel apprehensive on entering a mosque. The reverence expected in any place of worship leads one to fear causing offence through ignorance of custom. Outside tourist venues, such as the Blue Mosque in Istanbul, visitors might well be stared at, but in the UK there would be no opposition to their presence, provided they obey a few simple conventions. Guides or officials will determine who goes where, and direct visitors accordingly. The general rule is that men and women enter through different doors, and pray in different areas. Sometimes, the women sit behind a marked-off area at the back, and in other mosques they occupy a balcony. This segregation aims to ensure that worshippers' minds are not distracted from their duty to God.

Before entering a mosque, everyone, whether Muslim or non-Muslim, should be neatly and respectably dressed in something like their 'Sunday best', and a woman's head and arms must be covered. Too much make-up, scent (except *itr*), and skimpy clothing are all considered inappropriate; anyone wearing them may be refused entry. Both men and women remove their footwear, but not their socks or tights, though they can remove these too if they wish. Washing of the feet would not be expected of a tourist, but it would be considered very bad manners to enter a mosque with dirty or smelly feet. There are often taps in the wall, with stools beside them, so that people can wash their feet before prayers. There are also washing facilities in the lavatories in most mosques, which are separate for men and women. Sometimes there is a *loti*, a jug with a long spout, as well as washbasins and towels.

Today, many mosques welcome visitors, even if they are only entering the building out of interest in architecture, but this tolerance is not universal. In some places, such as Jerusalem, Damascus, and Istanbul, tourists are part and parcel of everyday life, but other mosques do not permit non-Muslims to enter, such as those at Mecca. A stranger going to the mosques in Whitechapel, Bradford, or Burnley might be looked at by some Muslims with suspicion, so visitors are best advised to first ask politely whether visitors are welcomed into any particular mosque, to respect prayer times.

CHAPTER 9

Come to the house a pilgrim

The physical building of the mosque may be of relatively low importance to Muslims, but Islam holds sacred as many places as any other world faith. As with Christianity or Judaism, Islamic shrines have for centuries been a magnet for pilgrims all over the world. Of all the sites sacred to Islam, one stands out as by far the greatest. Mecca, for all Muslims, is the ultimate pilgrimage destination. Mecca is the holy city where the Prophet Muhammad was born and lived, and as such is the epicentre of all things Islamic.

The *hajj*, meaning literally 'to set out for a place with a purpose', is now widely known as the annual pilgrimage of Muslims to Mecca. People who care nothing for Islam still use the term 'Mecca' as a synonym for an ultimate goal, or a place that someone aspires to visit. Mecca is so holy that it is forbidden for non-Muslims to enter the city. Consequently, it is hard for any non-Muslim to appreciate its significance. Photographs of massed pilgrims circling the *Ka'ba* do little to communicate the raw emotion that the *hajj* stirs in Muslims making the pilgrimage. So-called

71

infidels are excluded from what is the biggest annual mass movement of people on the planet. Last year four million Muslims made the pilgrimage to Mecca, and it is estimated that during the past 70 years more than 30 million pilgrims have travelled to Saudi Arabia for the event. So, what is it about it that is so special, that draws so many Muslim pilgrims there every year? In order to get to grips with this question, it is firstly necessary to understand the motives, influences, and sacrifices involved in any pilgrimage.

The concept of pilgrimage itself is not exclusive to Islam, but predates the faith, just as it predates Judaism and Christianity. There is evidence as far back as prehistoric times of tribes who had moved away from their place of origin journeying back periodically to pay tribute to the gods who had watched over their early years. The concept of pilgrimage is rooted in the idea of local gods. Those who were living in the plains returned to the mountains from whence they or their ancestors had come; those from the rivers went back to the desert. These journeys were more than nostalgia: the pilgrims were giving thanks to a deity, honouring him or her, and paying tribute.

The desire to revisit a place of spiritual significance is arguably an essential characteristic of human nature. It seems natural that pilgrimage should be dedicated to a deity directly linked with that character, and that has often evoked a sense of celebration and joy. Ancient Egyptians regularly traveled to the place of the cat god Bubastis. The annual festival at Sekmet's shrine not only provided a focus for worship, but was the excuse for Bacchanalian celebrations, during which large quantities of wine were drunk, music was played, and there was dancing and general merriment. Egyptians had pilgrimages to Thebes; and the journeys that ancient Greeks made to Delphi to consult the Oracle were made in a similar spirit.

Jews have always been enthusiastic pilgrims. Shiloh and Mecca were both popular destinations. After the temple was built in Jerusalem about 1000 BC, it became the principal site for pilgrimages. Visiting Jerusalem and the temple was made difficult for a few hundred years, but once Herod renovated it in the first century BC, mass pilgrimages began again. Once more there was a hiatus in Jewish pilgrimages after the temple was destroyed in the first century AD. But, even if the mass pilgrimages stopped, individuals have continued to make a point of travelling to Jerusalem to honour their most sacred site.

Since 333 AD there have been Christian pilgrimages to visit places mentioned in the Gospels, or to sites that are associated with the saints, holy men and women who are venerated. In Britain the principal places visited are Canterbury and Walsingham. Over the centuries, those inspired by St Paul have journeyed to Rome; those inspired by St James to Santiago de Compostela in Spain. The sick have traditionally visited Lourdes in south-west France. Pilgrimages have also been a feature of many Buddhist and South American religious cultures. Followers of the Buddha, for example – regardless of the season or any specific date – make an effort to visit Kapilavastu, where he lived as a child, Benares, where he began his spiritual journey, or Kasinagara, where he left this world. It is hard to imagine that any or all of these pilgrims would not have experienced the same feelings of piety, devotion, gratitude, joy and sacrifice as Muslims making the ultimate journey to Mecca.

Mecca was already an important religious centre before Muhammad was born, and hence long before Islam. Thus, the *hajj* not only celebrates the Prophet, but a more ancient story, that of the reunion and forgiveness of Adam and Eve. As the story goes in the Bible, so according to the Qur'an: Adam and Eve were the original human couple created from the division of the original soul. In the Qur'an, having succumbed to the temptation of Satan and been cast out of Paradise, they were separated from each other, and each was condemned to walk the earth alone, confused and in pain. As they realised the error of their ways, they asked God for forgiveness, which He granted willingly. Muslims believe they were reunited at a small hill known as the Mount of Mercy, Jabal ar-Rahman, on the plain of Arafat – the same hill on which Muhammad delivered his final sermon on his last pilgrimage. To this day Muslims believe that if they are at the same place on the ninth Dhu'l Hijjah, they can be forgiven for all their past sins and begin again.

The *Ka'ba* shrine is well known as the pivot of the *hajj* rituals at Mecca. Today it is regarded as the house of God in Mecca, since Muslims believe it to be a replica of God's house in the seventh sphere of heaven, where the heavenly throne is to be found. The black stone itself that lies within the *Ka'ba* is about a foot long, and considered sacred by Muslims. It is framed in silver and set at a height of about 5 feet in the south-east corner of the *Ka'ba*. The stone and the *Ka'ba* are in turn enclosed by the Grand Mosque (*al-masjid al-Haram*), which stands in an open courtyard.

For the past 4,000 years it has remained in exactly the same place, and has always been a place of pilgrimage since, according to Islamic tradition, the black stone came down from heaven and Adam placed it in the first *Ka'ba*. Muslims believe the stone was originally white, but was turned black by the sins of humanity.

Islam holds that Abraham was ordered by God to rebuild the *Ka'ba*, with the help of his son Ishmael, when, it is said, the Angel Gabriel took the stone out of hiding and gave it to Abraham to place in the new *Ka'ba*. The shrine continued to be an important part of Abraham's life and, as a result, influenced the religious life of his time. Pilgrims today still follow the precedent established by Abraham, and the rites instigated by him are the same ones now performed by Muslim pilgrims more than 2,000 years later. The essential features of the ceremony are barely altered, although the prayers uttered by the pilgrims as they proceed around the shrine, have evolved.

The *hajj* also celebrates Abraham's sacrifice of his son Ishmael. As in Genesis in the Bible, Abraham's obedience to God is sorely tested, but the Qur'an contains a slightly different version of events. In the Qur'anic version of the story, Abraham also has a dream in which God instructs him to sacrifice his son as a measure of Abraham's obedience to Him. According to Islamic tradition, it is recorded in the *hadiths* that Abraham, his wife Hajarah and son Ishmael were all visited by a stranger who Muslims believe was Satan in disguise. Satan attempted to change their minds, claiming that they were being misled and that it was the Devil, not God, who was asking the sacrifice of Abraham's son. All three resisted the stranger, and threw stones at him to force him to leave. As in the Bible's version of the story, God relents at the last moment, and instead of Abraham's son a ram is sacrificed. This event is remembered in the Muslim year at the end of the *hajj* as Eid al-Adha. In both versions, Abraham's barren wife Sarah is given a son of her own, named Isaac.

After Abraham and before the life of the Prophet, idolatry had been rife in Arabia. Pilgrimages at this time were not only an opportunity for prayer but were also used as an excuse to meet for other, less pious activities. Many pilgrims believed that men and women should approach God as naked as the day they came into this world. As they processed around the *Ka'ba* their behaviour sometimes degenerated into something like a Rabelaisian orgy. Nor was the *Ka'ba* itself treated with the respect that was due: it had been desecrated by adornment with various idols and graven images. The walls were covered by paintings and graffiti, and the *hajj* nothing more than a circus.

It is said that long before Muhammad became established as a leader and Prophet, he visited the Ka'ba where he performed the ritual circumambulation seven times, and took off his mantle and spread it on the ground. The story goes that on this he placed the stone, and kissed it. Then he asked a chief to come forward from each of the four main clans, to take a corner and lift it to the proper height, Muhammad himself guiding it into place. He insisted that any sacrificed animals should be offered to the poor, as had been the case in the time of Abraham; and returned a sense of piety, purity and austerity to the ritual. The lewd and unseemly practices that had formerly defiled the *hajj* now came to an end, the practices that had given the *hajj* a carnival atmosphere of frolic and frivolity having arisen out of ignorance and human conceit.

Muhammad insisted that every act during the pilgrimage should be a sacrifice to Allah, and be for Him alone. Muhammad not only outlawed the singing, drinking, and sexual excesses that had been a feature of the *hajj*, he also forbade the poetry competitions, which had previously been little more than a means by which pilgrims extolled their own virtues while denigrating the behaviour of their rivals. However it was much later, only when the Prophet made his final, seminal pilgrimage to Mecca in 629AD, that the *Ka'ba* finally restored to the state of piety for which it is now renowned.

Nowadays, every good Muslim hopes to make the pilgrimage to Mecca once in his or her lifetime. It is a duty to do so, if they are able, and a privilege to retrace the steps of the Prophet. It is so important that it is regarded as the fifth pillar of Islam. Although doing God's will and worshipping Him is the primary objective of the pilgrim, those who attend *hajj* also enjoy feelings of unity and pride: pilgrims are a part of a unifying and united force. Although successfully completing the *hajj* bestows on a Muslim the honorary title *hajji* (or *hajja*, for a woman), the sense of inner satisfaction is reward enough.

The pilgrimage itself lasts from the eighth to the twelfth of Dhu'l Hijjah, the twelfth and last month of the Muslim calendar. Many pilgrims set out several months ahead of time, in order to spend an extended period in the holy cities. Caring for the pilgrims – food, housing, guides, transportation, even sanitation and toilet facilities – is a major logistical challenge for the Saudi Arabian government, which allocates millions of dollars to the Ministry of Pilgrimage for this administration. Last year, nearly four million people visited Mecca. In 2011 they arrived in 6,226 flights into the new King Abdul Aziz airport at Jeddah, where the Hajj terminal receives ten jumbo jets at a time, met by 15,0000 buses. The pilgrimage is now so well organised that possession of a *hajj* visa includes the provision of guides and tents, as well as transport. Even 'zamzam', the holy water, is included in the cost.

Each Muslim is allotted to a group, and all groups are led by experienced guides. Once in Saudi Arabia, accommodation is arranged: there are over 43,200 tents pitched at Mina, and each will house around 40 pilgrims. Tents, like those that sheltered the British armies of the Raj, are equipped as if they were their temporary houses. But, unlike the tents of the Raj, electricity and water are laid on, and there are bathrooms and air-conditioning. The guides looking after the pilgrims number more than 2,000. Additionally, there are around 25,000 crowd control officers, who do everything possible to prevent the crowd becoming a stampede or crush. Even the best behaved will drop the occasional piece of litter – but there are 14,000 rubbish collectors waiting to pounce on it.

It was not always so organised in the past. Before the time of Muhammad, pilgrims would set off on the *hajj* without making any provisions for the journey. They would live a hand-to-mouth existence, even begging as they went for food and shelter. They assumed this would be evidence that God would always provide for the righteous; but in the Qur'an God does in fact state that making sensible provision for the *hajj* is one of the conditions of being a pilgrim. Although the best provision for life is piety itself, this does not excuse any pilgrim from being prepared for likely eventualities on his journey.

Making the *hajj* before air travel inevitably involved great personal sacrifice, but it has only ever been required of Muslims who could afford it. Even the rich had to sacrifice time, for the journey then could take years rather than months. For many others, the cost of the pilgrimage could eat up a lifetime's savings. Even now, despite cheap flights, a poor Muslim will have to save up to join the *hajj*. Very often family or friends club together so that one of their number may go to Mecca and represent them all. Older and or infirm Muslims, who are not fit to bear the stress of the trip, rely on the younger generation going on their behalf. The elderly often fear that their infirmity will prove to be a nuisance to their fellow pilgrims, but, even so, they don't question the value of taking part because of the thought that they might die while performing the *hajj*: it is an honourable end, and one treated with special reverence.

In God's eyes, it is not just the practice of pilgrimage that is valued, but the intention of going on the *hajj* is all-important. Would-be pilgrims still gain honour even if they are prevented from making the journey by some unexpected event. Some Muslims make the *hajj* several times, but as the numbers wishing to travel are so great this is actively discouraged. If a person pays for the *hajj* by dishonest means, this invalidates its spiritual significance. Although the intention to take part is what matters, once on the pilgrimage (and if the pilgrim is still fit) Muslims are required to carry out four duties. They must first enter the state of *ihram* and put on special clothes, which are the same for everybody; they must circle the *Ka'ba*; they should stand at Arafat; and, lastly, they must circle the *Ka'ba* once again.

Once in *ihram*, they conform to rules that are designed to purify them, both physically and spiritually. The purification rites, by removing any outward differences, make every person equal as they come before Allah. Pilgrims begin by taking a full bath. This is one of the few occasions on which Muslims forgo the pleasure they derive from scent. Since they are not allowed to use scented soap, unscented soap is on sale everywhere. Once they start on their pilgrimage, pilgrims are not allowed to cut their hair or nails: this is considered an interference with nature. So a great number of barbers are ready to cut the pilgrims' hair. At this time, they are also required to reaffirm their desire to join the pilgrimage. Men cast off their normal clothes, whether they usually wear suits, jeans, or South Asian *shalwar khameez*, and they put on fresh, white, seamless garments. All are identical so that none stand out as being richer or more powerful than their brothers or sisters before God. The social order is disguised and therefore forgotten.

Pilgrims' heads are always left uncovered as a mark of humility, but they are allowed to shade themselves from the scorching sun with an umbrella or parasol. Women can wear what they like, provided that it accords with Islamic law. They usually wear plain white, loose, long dresses and a veil. Every part of them is covered except for their face, feet, and hands. Rings and jewellery are discarded. Leather, like jewellery, is prohibited, but plastic sandals and belts are available for those who do not opt to go barefoot.

After passing *miqat* and saying a short *salat* (consisting of two *rak'as*), every Muslim is bound to be honest and pious, as a true servant of Allah. Sex is forbidden, as are any lascivious thoughts. Engagement and marriage are forbidden. Every Muslim's mind must be kept pure and at peace; every heart tuned to the will of Allah. A Muslim is required to be completely in harmony with nature, so no plant may be disturbed and no tree felled. No hunting is allowed, and no animal may be killed.

Once the pilgrims reach Mecca, they immediately go to the Grand Mosque. The Grand Mosque dwarfs St Peter's in Rome, and some would say it makes St Paul's look like a country parish church. On a single occasion, the Grand Mosque can hold enough people not only to fill St Peter's, but the Vatican Square outside. On the way to, and upon their arrival at, the shrine, Muslims recite the *talbiyah* supplication, in which they assert to Allah that they have arrived and are at His service. The prayer is the response to the divine call to pilgrimage. The pilgrim prays: 'At Your command, here I am, O God, here I am! At Your command I am here, O Thou without equal, here I am! Thine is the kingdom and the praise and the glory, O Thou without equal, God Alone!'

Upon entering Mecca, the Pilgrim recites another prayer: 'O God, this sanctuary is Your sacred place, and this city is Your city, and this slave is Your slave. I have come to You from a distant land, carrying all my sins and misdeeds, as an afflicted person seeking Your help and dreading Your punishment. I beg You to accept me, and grant me complete forgiveness, and give me permission to enter Your vast Garden of Delight.'

Unlike the congregation in Rome, pilgrims do not drift home or socialise after the service. Instead, they walk around the *Ka'ba*, circling it seven times anti-clockwise as an expression of the unity of God. As the pilgrims circle around the *Ka'ba*, a movement known as the *tawaf*, they all try to touch the holy black stone. Try as they might, it is difficult for over a million people to touch the stone, and most of them will have to content themselves with going through the motion, separated from it as they are by a milling throng.

When the Prophet founded Islam, one of the basic tenets was a ban on graven images. As pilgrims file past the stone, they show their understanding of the Prophet's edict by repeating the assertion of the Caliph 'Omar: 'I know that you are only a stone, that doesn't have the power to do good or evil. If I hadn't seen the Prophet kissing you, I wouldn't kiss you.' Pilgrims then have the opportunity to say their own private prayers at a place between the black stone and the door of the *Ka'ba*. They then say another prayer of two *rak'as* at the Station of Abraham.

The day is not over: pilgrims are now expected to perform what is known as the ritual of *Sa'i*. Each Muslim walks briskly or runs seven times between the small hills of Safa and Marwa, in memory of Hagar's search for water. Hagar had feared that both she and her child Ishmael were destined to die of thirst, and she ran to and fro in search of water. Islamic tradition holds that Ishmael kicked the dust with his heels. A spring of water erupted, and as it flowed it made a kind of gurgling noise that sounded to Hagar and Ishmael as if it was repeatedly saying 'zamzam'. Gabriel told Hagar that a great nation was to spring from her son's loins (i.e., Muhammad and his descendants). The spring saved their lives, and ever since the sacred spot has been known as the well of *zamzam*. It is a symbol of the soul's search for the source of true life. It represents the belief of a Muslim that when all hope is lost, God will still be at hand. The well itself still exists, with steps leading down to it beneath the courtyard. Pilgrims nowadays drink some of the water, and some dip their clothes in it.

At this stage, what is known as *umrah*, or the 'lesser pilgrimage', has been completed. Some Muslims will stop and return home at this stage, perhaps planning to complete the full *hajj* later in life. Men now either shave their heads or have their hair cut short. Women cut at least an inch off theirs. After this, they are allowed to wear their usual clothes.

On the eighth day of Dhu'l Hijjah, the pilgrims take another bath and put on *ihram* once again. While it is still light, they leave Mecca to return to their tents at Mina, which is about ten kilometers away. Those who are not staying at Mina may go directly to Arafat, which is about eight kilometers further away, and some 24 kilometres east of Mecca itself. These pilgrims are joined at Arafat the next day, the ninth day of the month, by the other pilgrims. Together, they carry out the most important part of the pilgrimage, during which they will finally make their stand before Allah. This involves standing for several hours between noon and sunset in the blistering heat of the sun on the plain of Arafat where they can be cleansed of their sin, just as were Adam and Eve.

Today the pilgrims' exposure to the sun as they stand at Arafat is regarded as a foretaste of the Day of Judgement. It is the zenith of the pilgrimage. The authorities have installed a system of sprinklers that deliver a refreshing spray of water from tall poles. This helps, but cannot relieve the baking heat. The men are bareheaded as they reflect on Allah and pray for His mercy. Muslims say it is a time of powerful emotions and feeling of spirituality, and that there is a feeling of being completely cleansed and a sense of release. It is certainly an extraordinary sight to witness two million Muslims performing the noon and afternoon prayers in total silence.

On the ninth day, once the sun has gone down, the pilgrims rush back to Mina and Mecca, saying their final two sets of prayers of the day, and spending the night at Muzdalifah. The following morning they collect small stones that they take to Mina. Once there, they throw seven of the stones at the largest of three pillars. The ritual is in remembrance of the occasion when Abraham was told by God to sacrifice his son Ishmael. The casting of the stones symbolises the conquering of Satan's temptations by Abraham, his wife and his son Ishmael when they had refused to believe him. Muslims hurl their pebbles (taking care not to injure anyone nearby) and rededicate themselves to the service of Allah, reaffirming their promise to drive the devils from themselves.

The next step in the pilgrimage also recalls God's call to Abraham to sacrifice his son Ishmael. It re-enacts the replacement of Abraham's son by a ram, commemorating Abraham's willingness to take his son's life in obedience to God. This can take place at any time on the tenth day of the month, when the sacrifice of a goat, sheep, camel, or cow is performed at Mina as a representation of Abraham's ram. Usually the head of the family sacrifices the animal in the approved method, and the meat is later eaten. This contrasts with the ancient pre-Islamic sacrifices at Mecca, when the blood of the animals was spattered on to the walls of the *Ka'ba* and their meat was hung around the pillars. Not every person buys an animal to make the sacrifice, since each animal provides ample meat to go around: some pilgrims make a donation instead. The meat is roasted and shared. This three-day feast is known as the Eid al-Adha, and all around the world Muslims make sacrifices to join the celebrations.

After the feasting it is time for the barber again. Men's heads are shaved, and women lose a lock of hair. Pilgrims put on their everyday clothes and resume all their usual activities, except for sexual intercourse. They then go back to Mecca for a second circling of the *Ka'ba*, the final *tawaf*, and only then is the pilgrimage accomplished.

During the final three days of the *hajj*, 11-13 Dhu'l Hijjah, any of the pilgrims who are still there cast seven pebbles at each of the three pillars at Mina again. Today, the task has been simplified by the building of a two-story ramp that allows large crowds to throw their pebbles without being crushed. On the twelfth day, the pilgrimage is over for everyone. Many pilgrims orbit the *Ka'ba* for a third time as a farewell gesture, and to make a final prayer, the *tawaf al-wada*, in which they pray that this should not be their last visit.

After the *hajj*, most pilgrims continue their visit to Mecca by visiting the tomb of the prophet in Medina, although Orthodox Muslims, including Wahhabis, largely of Saudi Arabian origin, discourage anything that might be interpreted as the worshipping of an individual. As the pilgrims go home, they thank God that they have been allowed to take part in the great festival of the Islamic year, a ceremony in which every Muslim throughout the world, and not only those on the pilgrimage, has taken part. It represents and demonstrates the spirit of unity and brotherhood that binds all Muslims together, regardless of their nationality, political views and cultural differences.

CHAPTER 10

Fast so that you may learn self-restraint

The acts of prayer and pilgrimage help Muslims to focus on their spirituality, as well as binding them together by allowing them to join in a shared religious experience. Likewise, fasting performs an equally fundamental role. It is so important to Islam that the great early Muslim theologian al-Ghazzali described it as 'one quarter of the Muslim faith'. As such, the act of fasting is known as the fourth pillar of Islam. It is not simply a matter of giving up food during the daytime. It is a symbolic act, enabling Muslims to rid their system of impurities on all levels and so become closer to God.

God's message to Muhammad was that fasting helps us to learn self-restraint, and it is an example set by the Prophet himself who, according to a famous *hadith* by Bukhari that describes the frugality of Muhammad, would break his fast with a sip of water and a date. To this day, many Muslims do the same. Through the physical act of fasting, Muslims experience the deprivation that the poor bear throughout the year, thus hopefully becoming more sensitive and responsive to their suffering as a result. This makes crash–dieting in the West, aimed at dropping a dress size in a few weeks, seem rather shameful.

Ramadan, the month of the fast, whose name comes from the Arabic root *r-m-d*, 'the great heat', from the soaring heat in the deserts of Arabia, is the ninth month of the Muslim calendar. It is special for Muslims as it was during this month that Muhammad received the call to be a prophet; and God himself instructed that it should be the official month of fasting, in a revelation received after the establishment of the community in Medina. Although no one knows the exact date of this, in the early days of Islam fasting took place on the tenth day of Muharram. This is still one of a number of days of voluntary fasting; but today Muhammad's call to be a prophet is celebrated on 27th Ramadan. This is a particularly significant night. Many people stay at their local mosque until long into the night, reading the Qur'an and praying. It is thought by some that prayer at this time is particularly powerful, awarding more blessings than prayers at other times.

Ramadan is about remembering to take nothing for granted, and about removing daily distractions so the mind is better able to focus on closeness with Allah. On a practical level, this means no eating, drinking, smoking, or sex from dawn to sunset for the entire month. In the wider scheme, while fasting it is especially encouraged that the believer avoids sin, such as lying, violence, greed, lust, slander, anger, and evil thoughts. The fast is about self-discipline, and a Muslim is called to make an extra effort to cultivate a more spiritual outlook.

The observance of Ramadan is regarded a source of blessing, and not a time of trial. Muslims generally look forward to this time of bodily and spiritual cleansing, and do not view it as being arduous or a chore. They hold it as a special period that brings them back in touch with the values at the heart of their faith. They see it as a healthy time, during which rich foods are avoided and their digestive systems can be rested and cleansed. At Ramadan, Muslims are given the opportunity to master all their natural appetites, mental, spiritual, and physical. It also allows them an opportunity to get together with friends and family, and to share their food after the hour of sunset. According to Islamic tradition, during this time the gates of heaven are opened, the gates of hell are closed, and Satan is put into chains. Hence fasting during Ramadan is considered thirty times better than at any other time, although many Muslims do fast at other times, some even on a weekly basis.

Ramadan observances do vary slightly from culture to culture, but most Muslims begin the fast, according to the Qur'an's instruction, at the moment when dawn makes it possible to distinguish 'a white thread from a black thread'. They then break the fast as soon as possible at sunset, eating a light meal later in the evening, with perhaps a final light meal in the early pre-dawn hours before the next morning's fast begins – but this all depends on local custom and personal preference. The evening is a time of relaxation, of visiting, prayer, and Qur'anic recitation. Printed Qur'ans divide the text into thirty sections to facilitate reading the whole book during Ramadan. Most Muslims accomplish this. Sounds of recitation often punctuate the evening air. Most individuals perform a voluntary *salat* of twenty *rak'as*, called *taraweeh*, sometime after the fifth prescribed prayer of the day. Most go to the mosque during the evening, especially during the last ten days of the month.

Muslims say that Ramadan demands a certain spiritual attitude towards the body. The hunger, supplemented by the prohibition on perfume and make-up, brings a Muslim back every year to what is regarded as a more natural state. Whether it be experiencing the hunger of the less fortunate, expiating one's sins, forgiving others theirs, renewing contact with one's nearest and dearest, or simply taming one's passions, a time of fasting is about reflection and contemplation; a return to the core values of Islam, and a reassessment of what it means to be a Muslim.

Since fasting can make people feel weary and weak, great care is taken over the type of food eaten during Ramadan. The consumption of special dishes at this time dates back to the earliest Islamic days, varying according to culture and region. In medical Islamic recipes *harira* is sometimes mentioned, and described as being made out of milk, flour, and fat, rather than being a broth. Early Muslim scholars such as Bukhari and ibn Hanbal talk of *harira* made of flour with cooked milk, and a broth generally made with bran and meat cut into small pieces and boiled in water. In the Muslim East, al-Baghddi's *Kitab at-Tabikh*, written in the thirteenth century, gives recipes for meat and flour dishes. In the Muslim West, ibn Razin gives nine recipes for soups and eight for *harira*, based on bread reduced to fine crumbs or on moistened flour slowly poured and turned into a broth of plain water and salt with oil, egg, or chicken, and flavouring ingredients such as coriander, ginger, cinnamon, onions, and garlic.

Nowadays, other sweet fruits such as dried figs and *halwa* supplement the dates, and snacks are sometimes eaten between night-time meals, especially biscuits and tea or coffee. A sign of the approach of Ramadan in the streets of North Africa is the transformation of doughnut merchants' shops into delicious *halwa* stores, though home preparation of *halwa* is still very common. *Halwa* consists of wheat flour, eggs, ground sesame, saffron, olive oil, butter, orange-flower water, vinegar, yeast, and a pinch of salt. These ingredients are mixed, energetically kneaded, allowed to rise, shaped, fried in oil, and then soaked in honey before being drained and dusted with sesame seeds. The resulting *halwa* is served with soup or with dry cakes and tea or coffee, as a snack.

In some cultures, such as in Morocco, special foods are prepared, including those of the *s'hur*, at which different kinds of pancakes are eaten, and those of the *ftur*, *harira* or soups, which are used to break the fast. On the eve of Ramadan, people prepare a honey cake to accompany the soup, known as *halwa*, *sellou* or *zammita* – sweet cereals and other dry cakes eaten as after-dinner snacks. Similarly, in Afghanistan special sweets and pastries are prepared, such as *halwa-e swanak, sheer payra* and *goash-e fil*. Stocks of these sweet foods are replenished during the third or fourth week of the month. *S'hur* marks the start of the fast, whereas *ftur* ends it.

If Muslims follow Muhammad's example during Ramadan, one would imagine their body weight to show evidence of it by the end of the month. However, the opposite is often the case. Some Muslims actually put on weight, owing to the increased consumption of sugar in the dates, and all the flour. Forty years ago, the *ftur* consisted of a bowl of soup preceded by 'a sweet fruit, a small amount of honey, or even just a mouthful of water', and it was thought that that alone gave the strength of a light meal. Ben Talha, writing in 1950, spoke of Muslims breaking their fast with toast with butter, or bread soaked in beaten eggs and cooked in butter, something like French toast. Now, in some circles, Ramadan is an excuse to host lavish parties every night and taste exotic foods not sampled since the last Ramadan.

Whatever cultural variances exist between customs at Ramadan, overall the month is seen by Muslims as a very special time. There is a feeling of camaraderie. The fast is a great leveller, and brings out the best in everyone, whether rich or poor.

CHAPTER 11

Every good act is charity

Fasting in Islam involves sharing with those less fortunate in society; but showing regard towards and helping others is not just for Ramadan. Nor does the concept of charity in Islam just concern money. Every Muslim is given a personal responsibility towards others, and this has wider implications. 'Every good act is charity,' said the Prophet Muhammad. 'Smiling upon your brother is charity, urging others to do good is charity. helping the blind is charity, removing stones, thorns and other obstructions from the road is charity.' Such acts of good will and kindness towards others reflect the kindness he showed to others in his own life. They are known in Islam as *saddaqah*, meaning literally 'righteousness', and are a testament to a person's faith; they are acts of goodness based on both free will and a desire to help others.

Such is the importance of charity in Islam that it is considered the third pillar of the faith. *Zakat* (derived from the word meaning 'to purify, thrive or be wholesome') is an annual charitable donation that all Muslims, rich and poor, are expected to give, although no one is forced, and no one checks. It is a moral decision that is left to the conscience of a person. Of a Muslim's worldly possessions, 2.5 per cent must be given as alms each year. By giving to those less fortunate, a person attains righteousness and virtue. Islam dictates that ultimately everything in the universe belongs to God. Our homes, cash, belongings, even the clothes on our back are only on loan from Him. If God has chosen to make a person rich it is His will, and their riches are only given in trust in order for them to be used wisely. According to the teachings of Muhammad, there is no use coveting worldly possessions or allowing greed to be your motivating force. Wealth should not be clung on to selfishly, but circulated and distributed more fairly around society for the benefit of all. Specific types of people should be assisted. 'Alms are for the poor and the needy, and those employed to administer the funds; for those whose hearts have been reconciled to truth; for those in bondage and in debt; and in the cause of God; and for the wayfarer.'

Since Muslims have a responsibility to help and support others, first and foremost they have a duty to look after their families and dependants. This applies to all Muslims, not just the men, and refers equally to the idea of emotional supportiveness as it does to financial and material protection. The popular image of the Muslim man going out to work and bonding with other men while the women of the family remain behind at home behind closed doors may be a fair representation of the situation in most parts of the Islamic Middle East, especially in those areas that have retained strict cultural traditions such as Iran, Saudi Arabia, Afghanistan, and parts of Pakistan, but it should not be forgotten that this is cultural tradition, and not hallowed by the Qur'an. Khadija, the Prophet's first wife, not only worked, but was a highly successful businesswoman. In several Muslim countries, including Turkey, those in the Balkans and in North Africa, women work just as they do in Britain and other countries.

Few wage slaves on the commuter train into London think of the week's work ahead with much beside apprehension. It is a chore: a burden that must be borne to support a family or lifestyle. But there was a time when work was a pleasure as well as a duty. The axiom was that if someone was not enjoying their job, and was no longer proud of the part it played in providing for the neighbourhood or the country, it was time for them to give it up and to move to something else. Originally, in Western Europe, and perhaps too in the United States, a somewhat romanticised code of ethics governed industry and commerce. In any organisation, the first consideration of those who managed it was the client or customer. Second was the welfare of the staff; and third, workers and their bosses had to remember that it was their responsibility, in addition to producing a worthwhile product or providing a good service, to make a reasonable profit for their shareholders.

That is no longer the case. No longer does the management build up a company so that it may represent a valuable part of society. Now the primary aim is to trade at a healthy profit, regardless of whether the company is providing a good service or product for the general public, so that it may be sold to the huge advantage of those who have been running it. The old order of customer before staff, and staff before shareholder, has now been reversed: the priority is now the future of the shareholders and managers, with customer satisfaction second (because without it the share value would fall); and the staff are rarely considered at all. Given, as many see it, a lack of an ethical approach or any integrity in the Western business world, the Islamic attitude to commerce can be seen as a refreshing alternative.

Islam teaches Muslims not to regard work just as an inevitable burden. It is an essential feature of everyday life. Muslims should take pride in what they do, and regard their employment as one means by which they live a good and prosperous life. Unlike Christians, who may fear that they will never go through the eye of the needle if their shop, factory or bank does well, Muslims do not see the opportunity to make money as anything shameful. They thank God that they have returned a good profit on the week or month's business. A Christian, it sometimes joked, might seek God's forgiveness for having done so well. Wealth to the Muslim is not a sign of sin, but an indication that a man has worked hard and taken advantage of the chances that God has granted him. God has rewarded him for his efforts.

The Islamic approach to work is that everyone should use the opportunities and abilities that Allah has given them to their fullest potential. No work is despised or looked down upon. Labouring, in the eyes of Allah, if that is what someone is fitted for, is just as praiseworthy as white-collar work. Muslims make the assumption that if someone has a gift, whether physical, creative or commercial, it is their duty to use it so that they don't become a nuisance and burden on others. As everyone has something they can offer society, there is little excuse for remaining unemployed. Allah is compassionate, and so the Qur'an expects His children to follow His lead. If someone is unable to work because they suffer from some terrible disability, is ill, or is burdened with some unavoidable misfortune, unemployment would be acceptable. But even so, begging is not condoned. It may be morally permissible in the Western world, where it is often considered as evidence that someone has suffered misfortune. However, unless there is particular reason to believe that this is so, the Islamic attitude might be that the person has simply failed to make the best of their capabilities.

In non-Islamic society, the law of the land determines the rules of business, but it is quite another ethos that determines exactly how Muslim businesses are conducted. All business owners, shareholders, managers and employees are responsible not only for obeying civil law, but, more important, but for obeying the law laid down by the Qur'an. Islam holds that all work should be respected, provided it does not disobey the Qur'an's teaching. If the work involves dishonesty, is dishonourable, or if it is dependent for profit on moral laxity or indecency, it is contemptible and condemned. The Qur'an makes a clear distinction between lawful (*halal*) and unlawful (*haram*) work. Any form of business activity that is dependent on selling alcohol, which provides sexual services, or which offers facilities for gambling is illegal.

Business deals should always be based on the principles of freedom and justice. Freedom suggests that there has been no coercion of those involved, and justice requires that the deal be a fair one. The Qur'an gives details that can be used to judge whether these standards have been met. The businessman or woman must be sincere and honest. When the transaction is being negotiated, it is a firm rule that at all times those involved must display impeccable manners and never show signs of anger or ill-temper. The Qur'an praises those who run their businesses successfully, are fair towards their clients and customers, and who conduct a generally honest business. This is coupled with frequent exhortations to be fair in all bargaining. Few sins are criticised more acutely in Islamic countries than any cheating in business. Islamic teaching forbids making money out of dodgy deals. These are considered no better than theft. Nor, when making a contract, may anyone take advantage of an infirmity or weakness.

The fastest growing sector of the Islamic business world in the West is Islamic finance, now worth over $500 billion, with an annual growth of 15-18 per cent. Islamic banks can offer an invaluable service to Muslims without contravening the strict and detailed Islamic laws that govern finance, and, via a slightly complicated sidestepping of the usual rules of banking, seek to accommodate Islamic prescriptions about looking after someone else's money. No banker is allowed to benefit by charging interest, but they can charge for banking services, or take a cut of profit attributable to the loan. Though the Qur'an forbids usury, Islamic law accepts that money has to circulate. A nation's wealth cannot remain locked away in vaults, but needs to be invested in industry. So the tax laws in Islamic countries are weighted so that there is a disadvantage in keeping money in banks rather than circulating it.

The Qur'an does nothing to discourage the enthusiastic approach of Muslims to establishing thriving businesses that make a good, but always fair, profit by providing a good service. There are at least fifty references in the Qur'an extolling the rewards that should come the way of those who work hard. A good work ethic is welcomed not only as a way of becoming successful in this life, and being able to support a family, but is also considered an advantage in the next. Islam teaches that there are three characteristics of a successful company. The person who has invested in it must have the ability to know whether it presents a worthwhile investment (one that has a good chance of offering a return). They must also be confident that they have the judgement necessary to make the correct decisions in its running. Finally, they should be prepared to run the business according to the rulings in the Qur'an.

There is an expectation that employers will ensure that their workers are treated with respect. Employers should not be arrogant, aggressive, or overbearing. Respect refers not only to man management but also to working conditions: office buildings or factories must always be comfortable, their facilities up to scratch, and the work schedule reasonable. Employees should not be exploited by overlong hours without breaks, and without concern for their health and welfare. Employees have the right to know what their wages are and what they must do to earn them. They must be paid promptly, as the following *hadith* (by ibn Majah) expresses: 'Give the worker his wages before his sweat dries.'

CHAPTER 12

Life after death

If Muslims pray, fast, and act charitably towards others, they will hopefully reap the rewards in the life to come. Living well in this life is crucial since Muslims believe there is only one mortal life, preparation for an eternity in Paradise at its conclusion – subject, of course, to the virtuous execution of the former. Unlike Buddhists, they do not believe in reincarnation. Hence man's guardianship of everything in the world during earthly life is temporary, and therefore all the more precious, part of a collective responsibility that must inevitably come to an end at death. Islam holds also that what can be seen in this world is just the tip of the iceberg as far as God's creation is concerned. After death the soul of a person may experience the reality. A good person is allowed access to heaven, whereas a bad person is destined for a much more unpleasant fate. There is no purgatory in the Christian sense, since all are imperfect and must be purified before entering heaven. Rather, the grave itself represents an antechamber of sorts. It is a prologue to heaven, as mortal life was to eternal life. There does exist an intermediate abode, *Dar al-Barzakh*, mentioned in the Qur'an, but it does not perform the same function as purgatory.

The promise of a heaven of some kind encouraging those on earth to conduct their lives in a virtuous fashion is, of course, not exclusive to Islam. Until the end of the nineteenth century, the belief in eternal damnation for the wicked and the existence of a heaven for the godly was as well established in other faiths as it was in Islam. As religious fervour has declined in the West, so has the profile of heaven in personal belief systems. In modern secular Europe, and arguably to a lesser extent in America, the hope of heaven and the threat of hell no longer exert the influence they once did. Yet strong beliefs about the life after death persist in the Islamic world, as important now as they were 1,500 years ago, perhaps even more so. Over 300 verses of the Qur'an and hundreds of the *hadith*s deal with the afterlife. Although these references vary in specificity and purpose, and interpretations of them differ, the importance of heaven and hell is not up for debate.

After death, Muslims believe we will all eventually face a Day of Judgement, when all good deeds and bad will be weighed against one another. A Muslim's ultimate fate is determined by which weighs heavier. It is said that good deeds weigh more than bad – that is, that God is more impressed by good deeds than displeased by bad – but only God knows the precise balance, or the weight of good required to merit entrance to Paradise. This concept of weighing up has led many Muslims who, for example, have a job that prevents them from fulfilling their commitment to daily prayers, to 'make up for it' – perhaps by giving extra *zakat*, or by volunteering for Islamic charitable organisations, though opinions differ on the effectiveness of this credit–system strategy.

Apart from the Qur'an, there are many early Islamic accounts of the process of death, heaven and hell, and the final Day of Judgement, which emerged early on after Muhammad's death. Such accounts were based on the Qur'an and *hadiths*. While such descriptions themselves are thought by many Muslims to be symbolic, they paint a vivid, colourful, and very detailed picture. Among them are the epistles by the *imam* Ibn Ahmad al Qadi and by the sheikh Jalaluddin al Suyuti, two exceptional documents that are much quoted from. Each contains slight variances in the actual description of the process of death and what happens afterwards, but essentially death is said to consist of two stages. The first is that of death itself, and time spent in the grave. The second stage includes the sounding of the trumpet and the resurrection from the grave to final judgement and final resting place. Before death, a leaf with the name of the person who is to die falls from the tree beneath the throne of God. From this sign, Isra'il, the Angel of Death, knows the appointed time has come. The length of an individual's life, indeed the length of time the universe will exist, is decided by God.

When someone dies, it is said that Isra'il appears to him. He and Satan have recorded the person's good and bad deeds. Isra'il is responsible for extracting the soul from the body. Satan then attempts to persuade the dying person to abandon his or her faith, perhaps offering water to alleviate discomfort. Having (hopefully) resisted Satan's entreaties, the dying person is confronted with a grave – a place of darkness and isolation. The discomfort of the grave usually lasts no more than forty days, but just as sin is universal, so is the punishment for it. No one in this world is perfect, and everyone – other than martyrs and prophets – is punished by having to experience some time, however brief, in the grave. While here, the dead catch glimpses of future rewards in Paradise, or, depending on their past behaviour, the torments of hell.

It is then time for the soul to attempt the journey to the seven heavens, provided it has not been condemned and denied entrance. In the case of condemnation, the soul is reunited with the body in the grave whilst also sent to hell. The bleak isolation of the grave, far from the seven heavens, is in some traditions the definition of hell: to be far from the grace of God. Having ascended from the earth, the dead person is then interrogated by two angels, Munkar and Nakir. They appear black, with piercing blue eyes. A question, which presumably requires the *shahada* to be given as its answer, is put to the disembodied soul: 'Who is your lord?' Martyrs and prophets are excused this step, and proceed directly to heaven.

One contentious area of Islamic theology concerns the souls of young children. One might assume it was obvious that a young soul would be 'fast-tracked', having had little opportunity for misdemeanour. Most of us understand the principle of a *tabula rasa* as implying innocence. Not so in Islam: in fact, the question of young souls is vigorously debated among Muslim scholars. The Qur'an offers no clear guidance, but the most widely accepted interpretation seems to be that infants (prepubescent children of Muslims, good or bad) go straight to Paradise, whereas older children share in their parents' fate – which seems a little unfair on the unwitting child of a sinner. There is no indication given about the children of non-Muslims.

With no purgatory, there is no waiting room for those unable to gain access to heaven through no fault of their own. There is mention in the Qur'an of people who have reached the 'heights', the sought-after position in the barrier that divides the righteous from the damned. They are able to see and recognise those whom they knew in the earthly life suffering the torments of hell and its fires. Likewise they may look to heaven, and see those who have obeyed the law enjoying the pleasures that are their reward. Whether the innocent damned are given this 'privileged' position (as near to limbo as the Islamic picture comes) is not clear. A book, recording the dead man's deeds during his lifetime, is affixed to his neck at the moment of death. At judgement, it is removed, and handed to him. He will know his destiny at this moment: if he is bound for hell, the book will be given to him in his left hand; if he is admitted to heaven, he will have it in his right.

The bridge that leads to Paradise is also the bridge above hell. To the damned, the way is hard, and those who travel it are likely to fall off into the hellfire that the bridge arches over on its way to Paradise. To those who have sinned, the bridge may be rough and uneven, or its surface as sharp as a sword; it may be so narrow that the sinner falls off immediately. But for the righteous – those who have led lives of obedience, virtue and charity – the bridge will appear as a wide thoroughfare, which is easy to traverse. The Prophet Muhammad waits to greet them at a pond on the other side. It should be said that most Muslims believe that those who have fallen are not necessarily abandoned for all eternity. Eventually, they too will experience God's mercy, be saved, and go to heaven.

As with Christianity, there is an exception to the rule of God's ultimate mercy. Jesus said the only sin from which one cannot be saved is 'the sin against the Holy Spirit'. He never explicitly tells us what this is, but it is supposed, variously, that he means denying the Trinity, blaspheming against the Holy Spirit, or falling into despair. Despair is the worst possible state for the Christian, since from despair there can be no salvation: if I have no hope, how can I be redeemed by God's love? For Muslims, the worst possible sin is quite similar. It is hypocrisy. Those who pretend to follow Muhammad's teachings, but oppose him in secret, reside in the lowest level of hell. For them, there can be no salvation: what matters is what is in one's heart.

Islam has given us an intoxicating and minutely detailed guide to the afterlife, in contrast to Christianity, which discusses heaven in rather more general terms. The Islamic heaven is a place unconstrained by earthly rules: everything is *halal*. The Christian heaven comes across as very much asexual, concordant with the general abnegation of natural sexual impulses that characterise that religion. Christians may well envy the Muslim, who, it is said, will enjoy ecstasy.

Heaven is described fundamentally, in both the Qur'an and the *hadith*s, as a state that is beyond comprehension or imagination. The Qur'an says, 'No person knows what is kept hidden for them . . . as a reward.' Heaven has seven spheres, or layers, the same seven heavens that Muhammad ascended through on his famous Night Journey to Jerusalem. God presides over the company of all these heavens, and the faces of those fortunate enough to reach Paradise light up under his divine influence. It is said by Muslims that so great is the pervasive and inexhaustible joy that the angels, the trees, the birds, and the rivers share in divine rapture. All are illuminated by it. On a metaphorical level, heaven is frequently referred to in the Qur'an as a beautiful garden – an image of Paradise as a garden recurs throughout the major world religions, especially in those whose roots can be traced to civilisations in harsh, desert regions. The Garden of Eden is the most familiar and obvious example, and *Firdaus* is a Persian word that eventually came to mean 'paradise', but originally meant a garden or small park. In the early Greek translations of the Bible, the term was used to describe the Garden of Eden.

Paradise is seen as vast, with a complex structure. There are eight heavenly golden gates encrusted with emeralds, diamonds, and rubies. The first gate is inscribed with the *shahada*, 'There is no God but Allah, and Muhammad is his prophet,' and also with, 'Through this gate enter the prophets, the martyrs, the tender-hearted.' Through the second gate, equally fine and richly ornamented, enter those who have obeyed the laws of purification, and have said their prayers daily in a well-regulated manner. The third is reserved for the generous-hearted, who have been prepared to give away to charity those things they hold dearest and most desirable. They are the alms-givers. Through the fourth gate proceed those who have been able to lead others to a righteous life. The fifth gate is for those who have with self-discipline controlled their desires and passions. The sixth is for pilgrims, and the seventh for those who fight for the faith. Through the eighth gate pass the pious men who have been discreet, have performed good works, and have not looked covetously upon those they desire. In Suyuti's account of the gates of heaven, the gates are equally rich, but their architectural details differ.

Whatsoever treatise is read, there is consensus among authors that, above all, Paradise achieves a reconciliation of man with nature. The Islamic conception of Paradise is a lush garden, described in the Qur'an as a beautiful oasis of calm. The trees of Paradise have inspired writers through the ages. Their leaves are always green and their branches always vigorous. In some accounts they are made not of wood, but of precious stones, their leaves of silk. The Tuba tree, the archetypal tree of Paradise, is described as having a trunk of pearl and 70,000 branches of topaz that reach up to the skies. In Paradise, one branch of a tuba tree shades every room and every dome. The other trees in Paradise are equally ornate: at the base of some of their trunks are winged horses, saddled and bridled and encrusted with pearls and hyacinths. The scent of Paradise is an exotic mix of musk, ginger and aromatic amber. The grass that grows there is coloured a bright saffron, and the broad rivers that flow through it provide water in abundance.

The Qur'an's description of Paradise inspires every earthly Islamic garden, and its shady trees and cool, trickling water contrast sharply with the reality of harsh desert and the unending arid plains of the earth beneath. An imitation or homage to the celestial garden of Paradise, recreated in an otherwise hostile landscape, gives hope and comfort to all travellers. The Paradise that the righteous will enter on the Day of Judgement – a garden divided by rivers of water, milk, wine, and honey – is mirrored by the cool tranquillity of the fountains, and the scent of the foliage and sweet-smelling flowers in an Islamic garden on earth.

The influence of such descriptions has undoubtedly had a profound effect throughout the centuries. Around these earthly mirrors of the heavens, an entire religious vocabulary has sprung up. In Persian, the word for paradise is the same used to refer to a garden, whether on earth or in heaven. The garden on earth is viewed as part of complete and perfect creation, treasured both for itself and as a reflection of heaven. It is both a blissful private setting in which to relax, and a reflection of the perfect symmetries of the cosmos: a place for contemplation, and a symbol of the perfect union of the earthly and the divine. The great Islamic poets saw God's beauty in the garden, and drew upon the images of its trees, plants, flowers, and birds to reflect the character of man, and the emotions and intricacies of his soul.

By the tenth century, the Sufis had begun to ponder the analogies that exist between man, nature, and the divine. They also drew on the metaphor of the garden, with its plants and flowers, to describe the complexities of the human soul. Each spring, the dead earth comes to life again with green shoots and buds, as, on the Day of Judgement, dry bones live again. Shibli, the eccentric tenth-century mystic of Baghdad, saw his fellow Gnostics in terms of the plants and flowers in the garden, and compared them to the spring. Such was the influence of the Islamic conception of heaven and hell that it spread far beyond Islamic society. It is said that even Dante was aware of the Islamic accounts, and was influenced by them in writing his *Divine Comedy*.

In Paradise there is not only water, but milk and honey. There is wine too, and the wine can be drunk without producing inebriation. Just as in Paradise it is possible to drink a limitless amount of wine without becoming drunk, so can those who are there enjoy as much fine food as they desire, for fortunately, the inhabitants of Paradise are spared the inconvenience of a digestive tract. Most famously, the pleasures of Paradise include the *houris*, to which the Qur'an refers specifically in a few passages, and the *hadiths* in many. The word itself refers to whiteness: in Paradise, as in the earthly world, this is a symbol of purity. It is also associated in Arabic with gazelles, which were an occasional and much sought-after addition to the desert.

Houris are ethereal women, characterised by beautiful black eyes set against fair skin. These women embody, yet transcend, the idea of feminine sexuality, representing the pinnacle of female attractiveness. Some accounts describe bodies made of saffron, musk, amber, and camphor, and hair of raw silk. These are most likely allegorical descriptions, intended to suggest beauty and riches. These perpetual virgins have fine flesh that seems translucent, and their faces have been likened to crescent moons. The simile is extended to even cover a *houri*'s spittle: were a *houri* to spit on the ground, the place on which she spat would immediately be turned into musk. Written across the breast of a *houri* is the name of her husband, linked to one of the ninety-nine beautiful names by which God is known. The *houris* wear gold bracelets on each arm, rings on each finger – and also, fashioned from precious jewels and fine pearls, on each foot. Each *houri* is deeply in love with her husband, and every man is a husband to seventy *houris*, in addition to the wife, or wives, he has been married to on earth. They live in pavilions with seventy beds, attended to by 70,000 maids of honour and a thousand slave girls, each one holding a bowl from which to feed the women and their husbands. The men's faces are reflected in the faces of their wives, and likewise the faces of the women are reflected in those of their husbands. Men undergo subtle changes in Paradise: whereas in life their beards were a symbol of virility, in Paradise their cheeks are hairless, and the only hair on the body is that of the eyelashes and the hair on their head. With each passing day they grow more beautiful, and their sexual potency and prowess increases. Men not only enjoy the company of the *houris*, but can remain united to their earthly wives – and so continue their marital life in Paradise if they ask for them. Neither a man nor a woman is compelled to have more than one wife in heaven if they choose not to. The point of the *houris* in the Qur'an is to make men and women aware that if they do good in their earthly lives they can live the life of a king or queen in heaven and have maids or male servants at their disposal should they wish.

A modified version of this image of Paradise has been used as an enticement to young Islamic men to lay down their lives in the fundamentalist battle against the West. Received wisdom in the West tells us that Muslims believe God has promised young recruits to the cause an accelerated journey to heaven and seventy virgins upon arrival. Serious Islamic scholars fairly unanimously reject this claim, explaining that it is based on a misunderstanding, or misquoting, of the holy texts. Others maintain that it is wrong to suggest that this would be an exceptional privilege – but only because all men in Paradise, not just martyrs, have seventy (or, by some accounts, seventy-two) virgins at their disposal. It goes without saying, of course, that such inducements to martyrdom are limited to extremists, and that the vast majority of Muslim scholars do not endorse the exploitation of the young and the intemperate.

Whereas those in Paradise enjoy a blissful time, their carnal desires satisfied and their love of beauty fulfilled, it is very different for the inhabitants of hell. The most persistent feature of hell in the descriptions from the Qur'an is fire, but the *hadith*s provide graphic descriptions of the many torments experienced in the different levels of hell. Hell, like heaven, has seven layers, each with its own gate and classification of sinner. Sinners are allocated to one of the seven levels according to the gravity of their misdeeds; the severity of the punishment varies from level to level. Muslims who believe in Allah, yet have sinned, will be in the uppermost level, and have the most immediate prospects of reprieve. Pagan infidels belong to the penultimate level. Religious hypocrites are to be found in the lowest level of all: whereas the believers on the upper level will ultimately be delivered by the gift of God's mercy, hypocrites can never hope to receive divine mercy. In contrast to the trees in heaven, the *zaqqum* in hell has devils' heads for flowers. Sinners are forced to eat its fruit, which burns their insides as if made from molten brass.

The Qur'an, normally rendered in more positive for-mulations, comes closest in its descriptions of hell to the tone of the Bible. The damned, we learn, boil in hot water, breathe in hot smoke, and are seared by biting winds. In his ascent into heaven, Muhammad, while still in the lowest level of heaven, espied the nature of hell. He learned how the bodies of the condemned fuel the hellfire. (No sooner have the damned been burnt, they are given a new skin – metaphorically, though no less painfully – so that they may experience the agony once again.) If the inhabitants of hell try to escape, they are pulled back into the pit with iron hooks.

The punishments of hell are fashioned so that they are related to the sin responsible for the person's damnation, again reminding us of Dante's account. Adulterous women who have given birth to illegitimate children are hanged by their breasts. Men who have committed the sin of adultery are forced to eat lean, stinking meat, while good meat is displayed beyond their reach. This is allegorical: the good meat represents the wives who were permitted to them on earth, while the stinking meat represents the women they wickedly desired and pursued.

The souls of men are not the only inhabitants of the afterlife. There are also angels, devils, and spirits (the *jinn*). The Qur'an specifically contains more than eighty references to angels. Though active in the earthly world, angels are created from pure light and belong to a formless, higher plane. They do not have free will, and therefore cannot sin. When Islamic texts mention the name of an angel they use a blessing that translates as 'peace be upon him' (often abbreviated in English to 'pbuh'). This blessing is also conventionally appended to Muhammad's name, and the names of the other prophets.

Islamic angelology has many parallels to its Christian counterpart. In both traditions, angels are the messengers of God (the word 'angel' is ultimately derived from a Hebrew word meaning 'messenger'). Angels have other duties, too: supporting the throne of God, guarding the walls between heaven and hell, and the gates to each level of both planes. They also act as guardians to mortals, and are responsible for recording men's deeds in the book that will be used in their judgement after death. There are angels in hell, too, described by the Qur'an as 'stern-faced, and utterly devoid of pity'.

As in Christianity, the most important angels are archangels: Gabriel and Michael are also important to Christians, but two others that feature in Islam are Israfil and Isra'il. Gabriel is undoubtedly the most important angel, in both the Qur'an and the Bible, though in the Qur'an he is mentioned by name only three times. It is Gabriel that Muslim tradition identifies as the unnamed angel who appears to Muhammad and leads him on his Night Journey to heaven. Gabriel also appears at a number of other crucial points in Muhammad's life: along with the Archangel Michael, he is one of the two strangers who remove the black spot from the heart of the infant Muhammad that symbolises his potential for sin.

Isra'il, as discussed previously, is the Angel of Death and third archangel. He is also mentioned in the Bible, and figures in Jewish tradition. Gigantic, with 4,000 wings and 70,000 feet, his body is covered with eyes and tongues. In his hands he holds a scroll upon which is written the names of every person alive, together with their destinies. The fourth archangel, Israfil, is similarly gigantic. He is the guardian of the human ability to think. Although he is not specifically named in the Qur'an, he is quoted in the *hadith*s as having feet beneath the earth and a head in the heavens. Like Isra'il, his body is covered with tongues, hair, and four wings that face north, south, east and west. He receives divine instructions written on a tablet held between his eyes, and relays these decisions to whatsoever angel is responsible for carrying them out on earth. It is Israfil who sounds the trumpet on the Day of Judgement.

The *jinn* (an Arabic word, from which we derive 'genie') are unknown in number, and invisible to the human eye. Belief in them predates Islam. They are capricious, and may cause good or ill to humans according to their fancy. Many cultures have troublesome or mischievous beings similar to the *jinn*: fairies, leprechauns, and trolls, for instance. Wheareas angels are made from light, *jinn* are made of the smokeless flame of fire. The Qur'an speaks specifically of a group of sinful *jinn* overhearing Muhammad preaching; this gave rise to a place at Mecca called the Mosque of the Jinn. The Qur'an tells us also that *jinn* helped King Solomon construct his temple at Jerusalem. Like fairies and goblins, *jinn* have their own kings and kingdoms. In pre-Islamic Arabia, they inspired the prophets, soothsayers and poets who had power before the time of Muhammad. Some even thought a *jinn* must have inspired Muhammad when he first claimed to have received revelations from God – a belief that was of course rejected by the Prophet himself, who was reassured by his wife, Khadija that the experience could not be the work of the devil. But bad *jinn* do exist in opposition to 'good *jinn*'. Known as the *shaytans*, these malevolent *jinn* are referred to many times in the Qur'an as they try to disrupt the thoughts of those at prayer.

Satan, often known as Iblis, is also mentioned many times in the Qur'an, though he has not the same significance in the Islamic faith. In Islam, he is not so much a superpower set in opposition to Allah as a troublemaker, something akin to the Norse god Loki; and he is not a fallen angel, as in Christian tradition. 'Iblis' comes from the Arabic *balasa*, 'he despaired', hence the name means 'he who causes despair'. Iblis was condemned because he refused to bow before Adam, but his punishment was delayed until the Day of Judgement. Iblis sows discord, discontent and evil in the mortal coil.

On the Day of Judgement Muslims believe God judges each person once again. The natural order is disrupted, the sky is torn apart, the stars scattered. The sun rises in the west and sets in the east. The seas rise up. Graves turn inside out and expel their occupants. Every soul now receives its final reckoning. This is the moment when they have to account for how they have made use of their creation by God and have honoured the gifts given to them by their munificent Maker. God's representatives ultimately triumph over evil, at which point a resurrection, or a redemption, begins. Israfil blows a trumpet to announce that this is the Day of Resurrection, and the world ends on its second sounding. After a time, God recreates the world, and with it the bodies of the departed. Muhammad, or one of the ancient prophets, is the first to reappear in the world, and then follows the resurrection.

CHAPTER 13

Family values

Before, hopefully, taking up their eventual place in heaven, all Muslims should lead a life that, if by no means perfect, at least aspires to maintaining traditional ethical and moral values that would not be out of place in any of the major faiths. Like Christianity and Judaism, at the heart of this aim is family. According to Islam, family forms the basic social structure that God intended for all human beings, and provides the stability of a healthy civilisation. It is the hub of all life, and an extended Muslim family provides a vital support network for all members. Nephews know their uncles well, cousins are like brothers, and the family is an entity that marches through life as one. If one of the family is in trouble, and needs help, there is no hesitation from comparatively distant relatives in coming forward to support, or even rescue, them. Family businesses in need of extra hands have a deep well of (sometimes reluctant, it is true) labour on which to draw.

Since a good and devout home life is essential to Islam, making a good marriage is of the utmost importance to all Muslims. According to one *hadith* by Baihaqi, Muhammad taught that, 'Whoever has married has completed half of his faith.' The Qur'an says, 'and among the signs of Allah is this, that he created for you mates, that you might live in tranquillity with them; and He has put love and mercy between your [hearts]. Truly in that are signs [about the nature of God] for those who reflect.'

Marriage in Islam is not about meeting and falling in love. It is not thought of as a union made in heaven between two perfectly matched people. It is a practical arrangement that brings both rights and obligations, and which can be successful only when these are respected and upheld by both parties. Family flows from marriage, and therefore any future wife is a potential mother and any husband a father. Non-Muslims may talk approvingly of how very much in love a young couple is, but in the Islamic world such mutual feeling is not necessarily seen as of particular benefit to a potential match. To a strict Islamic family, the state of being in love is regarded as a dangerous obsession that may lead the young couple to make foolish decisions. Muslim parents say it is important to have a clear head and understanding of the probable outcome of a union. Are the two young people likely to mature in a way that will lead to a happy and fruitful union, one that will last?

Idealised views of marriage belong in fairy-tales and Bollywood, say most Muslims. They argue that marriage is about responsibility, duty, sacrifice, and self-discipline, not about self-gratification and selfishness. It is a *mithaq*, a binding agreement between two consenting adults, in which both are ultimately answerable for their actions. It is a serious business.

In this contract, rights are allocated to man and woman, and the two separate roles of husband and wife are clearly defined. While the father is the head of the family and looks after it financially, the mother is seen to be the heart of it. A Muslim wife is chosen, among other considerations, according to her likely abilities as parent: it is expected that she would want to have children, as is that role that is regarded as the most important for a Muslim woman. As such she is the one responsible for setting the benchmark for manners and morality, and for seeing the children are brought up under the guiding principles of Islam. A Muslim mother is the pivot or epicentre of the family, and, as in societies all over the world, often acts as a buffer between father and children. She is the mediator where there are disagreements, and the peacemaker when there are quarrels.

This serious, practical approach to marriage is different from the experience of most non-Muslims, where there is not quite the same pressure to marry the so-called right person, an approach that existed among the better off in England until the end of the nineteenth century, when for most people questions of land rights and joint estates no longer became an issue. Today the majority of ordinary people are free to marry when their eyes meet across the proverbial crowded room. In the secular West, unmarried women live an independent social life before marriage, and find their husbands in singles bars as well as at parties. There has even been increasing acceptance of internet dating and chat-rooms. It has become socially acceptable for an unmarried woman to live as a partner with a man, without the assumption that they will one day marry. Her status would not, for the most part, be an object of disapproval; and for the past fifty or so years there would have been no question of social ostracism. She and her partner may now even have children together, and although the older generation of the family will not be pleased, they won't be outraged. The grandchildren will be accepted into the family circle. Women may choose to live by themselves, or with other people: it is a matter of personal choice and inclination (though single women may suffer from being regarded as possible competitors, and potential marital predators).

In many Islamic societies, a respectable family would be appalled if they thought that their sons and daughters were finding their future partners on the internet, and that the honour and future of the entire family depended on such a chance encounter. Often it is the older generation, in particular the parents, that discuss the potential of their children, relations, and younger friends and their likely compatibility. In many cases, the conclave – composed, as it is, of members of the family – selects a partner from amongst its own members. As a result, marriages between cousins are common. This practice has excited considerable comment, and some disapproval when Islamic communities have sprung up in Western cities and towns.

First marriages in Islam are frequently arranged by the families. The details vary according to culture, following matchmaking traditions that have lasted down the centuries. If there is no clubbing, and fewer unsupervised meetings between youths, there are fewer opportunities to fall madly in love with a stranger. Instead, discreet introductions are made over tea in the search for a suitable match. In Islam, young people have the right to refuse their proposed mates, but some trust their parents' judgement without question, and see their spouses for the first time at the wedding. All, however, have the right to refuse. Newspapers often write about arranged marriages between Muslims as if the partners were press-ganged. Yet forced marriage is contrary to Islamic law, and if it becomes apparent that undue pressure in any form was put upon the bride or bridegroom, the marriage can be dissolved as if it had never taken place. The reality of securing such an annulment, of course, is not as straight-forward as all that.

Islamic weddings are changing, and many wedding customs such as the bride's dress are matters of culture. Unique to all Islamic weddings, however is a display to family and friends by means of a *walimah*, an event that makes the marriage a public affair. If the wedding is low-key, the party that follows it rarely is. The Islamic prohibition against ostentatious displays of wealth is temporarily forgotten, and a wedding party can last for days. Expensive presents are lavished on the bridal pair. It is said that the splendour of the occasion ensures that the marriage between the couple is widely known and accepted. They have joined the social hierarchy, and have become part of the local establishment: this is to be celebrated and publicised.

Also compulsory is the question of a dowry, payable by a man directly to each of his future wives, not to their families (which is actually a Hindu practice). Thereby, once a Muslim woman has married into an established family, she has her own wealth. In Islam, this practice arose out of an interpretation of a verse from the Qur'an that requires husbands to take good [financial] care of their wives: 'And give the women their dower as a free gift, but if they of their own good pleasure remit any part of it to you take it and enjoy it with good cheer,' says verse 4:4. In some Islamic societies, the sum is very small; in others it is huge sum, and men end up saving for years, or marry very late. Although this practice has largely died out in Western secular society, the same principle was, and still is occasionally, found in Britain. When a woman with no money of her own marries into a rich family, it has often – certainly until the recent past – settled funds on her so that she has some degree of financial independence.

British history is, of course, filled with accounts of dowries. Nor has the practice always been confined to the aristocracy and landed families, where there was a natural desire to link estates. It has extended through all walks of life. Although the sums would not be as great, they were proportionally important. But it was the woman who was expected to bring a dowry into the family. Many of the greatest estates in Britain today would not still be in the family's control had it not been that sons married with a sharp financial eye to the fortune that would come into the estate's coffers as a result. In the early- and mid-Victorian era, the so-called new money of the Industrial Revolution provided an essential transfusion of cash that kept the big estates around the towns solvent. Later in the century, the value of marrying an heiress from the new world across the Atlantic was appreciated, and American money saved many British dynasties.

Where Muslims are concerned, once a couple has

married, Islam teaches that as the husband is head of the house, he is in command. In principle, this is no different from the promise made in the Christian Church in the marriage service until very recently – not only to love and honour, but also to obey. It was as if some form of military discipline existed in the household. The head of the house might be less able and less intelligent than his wife, but just as a senior officer took executive decisions, so did the husband. In Islam, if controversial decisions are made by the husband, there is theoretically a get-out clause for the wife. If the husband's orders contravene the instructions of the Qur'an, she is allowed to disregard them.

Husbands have a duty to look after their wives, to protect and care for them. As the Qur'an says, 'Husbands should take full care of their wives [with the bounties] God has given to some more than to others and with what they spend out of their own money.' Meanness within a marriage is as unacceptable to an Islamic household as authoritarianism underpinned with violence would be in a non-Muslim marriage. Even so, it should be remembered that a husband's tyranny was accepted in many sections of British society in living memory; and neither the Church nor the police would have interfered even if a woman were in danger of suffering significant physical harm.

As the idea of a husband as protector and provider for his family is taken very seriously in Islam, so in the Qur'an and *sunnah* there are many stipulations as to how a wife should behave. She should endear herself to her husband, and be keen to please him; never disclose his secrets; stand by him and offer advice; treat his family with kindness and respect; help him to obey God; encourage him to give charitably; make herself beautiful for him; be cheerful and grateful when she meets him: never look at another man; share his joys and his sorrows; be tolerant and forgiving; try to create an atmosphere of peace and tranquillity for him; and – after all this – she should be tolerant and wise. If a wife lives up to all this, she is the greatest blessing that God can bestow upon a man, and an incomparable joy in his life. As Muhammad himself said, 'This world is nothing but temporary conveniences, and the greatest joy in this world is a righteous woman.' If a wife can fulfill all Islam demands of her, she is surely worth every penny a husband spends on her.

Of all the virtues that the ideal Muslim wife should possess, perhaps the most contentious is her obedience to her husband. This aspect of Muslim marriage is one that many non-Muslims find reprehensible. Are their criticisms well-founded? Or are they easily explained by context and mitigating factors, as many Muslims maintain. Stories of wife-beating by Islamic husbands abound. A sanction stated specifically in the Qur'an, *surah* 4.34, remains one of the most, if not the most, controversial in the Qur'an: 'If you fear high-handedness from your wives, remind them [of the teachings of God], then ignore them when you go to bed, then hit [or overcome] them. If they obey you, you have no right to act against them.' Muslims defend this verse by saying we should refer to the sayings of Muhammad in order to put it into context. They argue that Muhammad himself never hit any woman, just as he did not beat a child, an old person, or a slave. What he did say was that a husband could not hit his wife and then expect her to share his bed that night. If a husband who went without blame discovered that his wife was conducting herself badly, and in a way that brought shame on them both, it was his duty as the head of the household to do something about it. Moderate Muslims argue that there is no proposal that a husband should hit his wife out of anger or disappointment. According to Islamic law if a husband bruised his wife he could be sued. Dr Ahmad Shafaat wrote that 'A wife has no religious obligation to take a beating. She can ask for or get a divorce at any time. If the husband beats a wife without respecting the limits set down by the Qur'an she can take him to court, and if ruled in favour has the right to apply for the law of retaliation and may have the husband beaten as he beat her.'

The question of polygamous marriages is one that perplexes many non-Muslims. Polygamy is regarded mostly with distaste and distrust by those brought up in non-polygamous societies, and it is often thought that polygamy has no role other than to satisfy a man's greater libido. Its disadvantages are apparent today in any culture that allows the practice. Muslims argue that rules surrounding multiple wives are designed to keep upset to a minimum. Officially, the eldest and first wife has to approve any new addition to the family. As each new wife is added, those who are already ensconced are supposed to give their approval, and the new wife's behaviour is monitored so that it won't cause disruption. Islam dictates that the wives have to be fairly and equally treated. They say it is a Western myth that the husband has to sleep with each of the wives equally often. No law can control his sexual desires, especially as he grows older. But it is laid down that the man of the house shall spend equal time with the different wives, including an equal number of nights – though how they pass the time together is not, and cannot be, prescribed. Financially, they are all supposed to be treated equally, just as good British parents will treat their children. All these points justify the practice of polygamy in the modern age; but the reality is that in many cases there are difficulties. Although the intention is that the wives should live together as a happy band of sisters, this is not always the case. Polygamy can be a recipe for discord and disaster. The first, and usually oldest, wife often resents her husband bringing another woman into the house; and younger women can frequently become jealous if one of their number seem to be acquiring the status of sexual favourite.

To properly examine the idea of polygamy in Islam, Muslims say that it is vital to recognise that pre-Islamic Arabia, long before the Prophet Muhammad was born, had been a polygamous society, and its acceptance into Islam was, in fact, a result of feelings of kindness and compassion towards women. As a result of the wars during the expansion of the Islamic Empire, or of early death from then-endemic diseases, women were frequently left widowed. Remarriage provided a better and more protected life, as well as financial security, for the widow. Although those women who did not remarry immediately after divorce or widowhood could return to their parental homes, there was the expectation that remarriage, even if polygamous, was a possibility, and that the family would not have to bear any financial burden for too long. If the woman was still of childbearing age, she had a much greater likelihood of finding another husband in a society that encouraged polygamy. But an older woman would often remarry, not only to avoid loneliness, but because her wealth or her connections were advantageous to her new husband.

In other cases, being a second or third wife meant that the woman could live her own life without the restriction of being her husband's only companion – thus, she might pursue a career, if she desired. Muslims argue that Islam has always used marriage as a means of protecting a single woman alone in society. As we have seen in Chapter 2, during his lifetime Muhammad gave instruction that it was the duty of a man to protect widows and older women without a family of their own. In many cases, the only way in which a man who had no sound financial background could establish his own *harem* was to obey the Prophet's instruction and find a rich, older woman whose money would support younger wives. The older wife then assumed a quasi-maternal role to the young wives, while being a 'sugar-mummy' to the man of the house. Polygamy, one way or another, was a cultural device that kept the number of single women in society to a minimum.

Although in our modern secular society it is hard to find comparisons to this scenario, if we look to times gone by an unmarried sister, who later became the younger generation's valued aunt, was an important part of family life. Few families were without single women, who spanned the generations and often became beloved figures in the households.

It often appears to non-Muslims that there is little respect for the single woman living in an Islamic society today. In the larger cities of the Middle East, some working women live alone, but most remain with their families until marriage. In strict present-day Islamic communities, a woman is regarded as a future wife until she is obviously too old to be of marriageable age. If widowed, and too old for remarriage, she is revered for the sake of her dead husband. Cultural considerations can often interfere with religious dictates. There, a single woman is welcomed readily into a private house, whereas an unaccompanied bachelor is considered with some suspicion, and as an obvious potential danger. Men regard another man's friendship towards their wives, sisters and daughters warily, and have doubts about their intentions. In some Islamic countries, if a woman resists the pressure to marry, and prefers to remain single, she must be prepared to live a life with little status – even if family honour requires her menfolk to protect her. Her social life will, accordingly, be restricted to family-centred or all-women occasions.

The life of the single woman in many Islamic countries has its obvious disadvantages, even misery, and is little envied. The Qur'an may affirm that 'wealth and children are not essential to earthly life', but the truth is that in most Islamic societies a woman who has not had children approaches old age with trepidation. In the Middle East, it is the married woman who enjoys prestige and high status, dependent of course upon that of her husband. These rewards more than compensate for the limitations and commitments of marriage and motherhood.

There are, of course, exceptions. In the twenty-first century, every Islamic country has women who have distinguished themselves in the learned professions, even if some remain unmarried. In some branches of Christianity in days gone by, a single or widowed woman sought refuge from the trials of the world by devoting herself to God and becoming a nun, but there is no equivalent for this in most of Islam – with a tiny number of exceptions. The unmarried women of the Mzab Berbers, who live in the Ghardaia region of Algeria, are group of Muslim holy women who have formed their own self-contained community, and have for hundreds of years, have taught religion, recited prayers on special occasions, and performed religious rites.

Children in Islam, as with any religion, are regarded as a blessing from God to any married couple. The man of the house in an Islamic family almost always still fulfils the patriarchal role, but despite a father's nominal leadership, the hub of the family in Islam has always been the mother. Non-Muslims used to the small nuclear family are sometimes surprised at the relationship between a father and his children in a Muslim family, in which mutual respect is perhaps a more prominent feature of the dynamic than intimacy. The role of the Victorian father as the head of the house has waned in the twenty-first century, and in its place there is often an easy friendship between parents and children, though not the deference found in a Muslim family. Nor is there always in the secular West the respect from the younger to the older generation that is arguably a cornerstone of Islamic life as laid down in the Qur'an: 'Your Lord has commanded that you should worship none but Him, and that you should be kind to your parents. If either or both of them reach old age with you, say no word that shows impatience with them, and do not be harsh with them, but speak to them respectfully and, out of mercy, lower your wing in humility towards them and say, 'Lord, have mercy on them, just as they cared for me when I was little'.'

Where a newborn baby is welcomed into an Islamic family, the common perception is that boys are often preferred to girls, but Muslims say this is a cultural matter, and against the spirit of Islam. Muhammad loved his four daughters, and praised any Muslim men who raised girls. Until Muhammad founded Islam, baby daughters had often been buried alive in the sand. The Prophet himself railed against the rejection of daughters: not only did he treat his own four surviving children, all girls, with tenderness and consideration, but he also harshly condemned infanticide. In Muhammad's words, 'Whoever hath a daughter and doth not bury her alive or scold her or prefer his male children to her, may God bring him into Paradise.' Muhammad also taught that education was to be as readily and freely available to girls as it was to boys.

It is, nevertheless, a tragedy that a girl being born today into a poor Islamic family in some parts of the Middle East may still not receive the welcome that would have been accorded to a brother. A baby girl may be deprived in a subtle, sometimes none-too-subtle, way from the cradle onwards. Poor mothers, anxious for another chance of bearing a son, tend to wean their girl babies early, because once they stop breast-feeding they are more likely to become pregnant again. So the daughter pays for her mother's ambitions by being underfed in the early months. Despite the Prophet's own approach with his female offspring, women in Islamic countries are likely to be disappointed if they do not produce a son. This is a largely cultural failing, rather than a religious one.

Since marriage and the family are taken so seriously in Islam, it is unsurprising that adultery is not tolerated. In the West, a blind eye used to be turned, so long as the liaison was discreet, and the pride of all involved was left as undamaged as possible. The situation has changed over the past forty years: adultery in middle-class circles is becoming as unfashionable as smoking. But even as adultery is becoming frowned upon, divorce is now more acceptable. The reasons for this are many and complex, but, in living memory society has so changed that divorce, which once would have resulted in social ostracism, is now accepted. The socially permissible way to reconcile this paradox is for adultery to be followed rapidly by divorce and remarriage.

The approach to adultery in Islam is very different. Adultery is still considered such a heinous crime that the just punishment for it is death. In the Qur'an, there is no specific mention of how the death penalty should be carried out, but the Qur'an does suggest that those who commit adultery are amongst the people 'who wage war against God and his messenger and strive to spread corruption'. Stoning has long been the most extreme form of punishment. It is not just women who are accused of, and punished for, adultery. If there is adequate evidence, a male adulterer is liable to suffer the same fate.

The full punishment for adultery is very rarely carried out. The problem, from the prosecution's point of view, is that the adultery needs to be witnessed by four people. There is a penalty if four people cannot be found to bear witness to the deed: whether a witness is right or wrong, if he or she cannot find three other people to support the accusation, they themselves are liable to be flogged. There is now an exception to this rule: positive DNA testing is considered as good a proof as the eyewitness account of four good and true people.

Muslim husbands sometimes also enter into temporary relationships or mini-marriages known as *mut'a*. Even though *mut'a* is not, strictly speaking allowed in Islam, its origins lie deep in history and it is still very much part of the fabric of Muslim life in the Middle East and Asia. The concept of temporary marriages dates from as far back as the Islamic conquests when initially they were introduced to govern the liaisons between soldiers separated from their wives by war, and the local women, and to make certain that any children born of the union were well cared-for. Later, the relationships between traders travelling in distant lands and the indigenous women were also covered by the same rules and customs. This was primarily to prevent rape, fornication and adultery among Muslim men when they travelled for hundreds of miles on foot and were sometimes away from their wives for years.

The contract in a temporary marriage is required to specify how long the liaison will last. These temporary marriages are not well regarded, often being thought of as being sleazy and secretive. They can last from a few hours up to ninety-nine years. There is no ceremony before the temporary marriage, but the contract is legally binding. The wife has no rights of inheritance, but the children from such a marriage are legal, and therefore share in the family inheritance.

The concept of temporary marriage dates back to a culture that accepted and made extensive use of female concubines. This contract between slave and master was not the same as a marriage document, and did not signify marriage, only ownership. Its stipulations were governed only by the good will of the slave or concubine owner. If a master and his concubine had children, her role and status would become that of what in Britain would be known as a common-law wife. Nowadays, however, Sunni Muslims regard temporary marriage as equivalent to prostitution.

Once a Muslim marriage is thought to have collapsed, and to be beyond rescue, notice of divorce is given. On three different occasions, over a period of three months, a husband has to declare his intention to divorce his wife, in order that the marriage may be dissolved and the divorce can go ahead in a straightforward way, without administrative complications. If, during this three months, the married pair is ever reconciled to the point where sexual relations are resumed, the divorce proceedings are considered to be over. The declaration of divorce is not allowed, or certainly not accepted, if the husband is out of his mind, or has been subjected to unfair pressure. It must be his decision and he must be conscious of its consequences. Insanity, drunkenness, or rages, are thought to so confuse the mind that a declaration of divorce made when a man is in any of these states is invalid. The woman cannot be given notice of divorce when she is menstruating, or has recently had a baby. The bleeding in both instances would, under Islamic law, make sexual relations unlawful, and it is thought that the unrequited libido of the husband might have undermined his better judgement.

The situation is different where Muslims are living in

countries where Islamic law does not prevail. Then the law of the land governs the question of divorce.

After divorce, a former husband must either continue to keep his wife, or let her go with kindness. But he must not keep her so as in any way to harm her or wrong her. Once she has reached the end of her waiting period (three months), he must do nothing to prevent her from remarrying. If a divorcee is breast-feeding, and her husband so wishes, he should continue to feed her, and maintain her in every way, including clothing her for two years, when the baby is weaned. No mother should ever suffer because she has had a child, and, likewise, the child should never be allowed to suffer because of the divorce.

The former husband is expected to provide a wet nurse if possible. Time may have altered specific interpretations of these rules, but the essence of them remains unchanged. Until recently divorce in Western non-Muslim society could result in hardship for mother and child. Every effort is now made to prevent this, but the difficulty has been to be fair to both parents. The Qur'an, if followed strictly, succeeds in being just, and ensures that no one is left destitute.

Although Islam lays down fair rules for divorce, it is a great tragedy that culture and tradition over the centuries have resulted in many injustices.

CHAPTER 14

Sex and sexuality

Sex is taken very seriously in Islam, but not in the way you might imagine. It is not regarded as shameful, nor is it proscribed or stigmatised. A healthy sexuality is to be enjoyed and respected. According to Islam, sex is a gift from God. It gives the believer a foretaste of Paradise on earth. There is just one stipulation: God's law requires that all sex be within marriage. Once married, all are free to pursue a full and satisfying sex life. Sex is normal, healthy, and to be encouraged between man and wife. There is nothing wrong in celebrating that gift, just as other gifts from God are celebrated.

Marriage is regarded as a divine privilege that allows men to reproduce, to provide comfort and pleasure to their women, and to achieve their own satisfaction. As the continuation of the family line is the purpose of sexual intercourse, it should be carried out with all the joy, exaltation, and intoxication Muslims conceive of as being at the heart of creation. They believe that, within marriage, sexual pleasure brings mankind closer to God. The Qur'an says that, 'Having sexual intercourse with one's wife is *sadaqah* (literally, loving charity).' In Muhammad's words, 'When a husband and wife share intimacy, it is rewarded, and a blessing from Allah; just as it would be punished if they had indulged in illicit sex.' The thought that a man and wife could live together without consummating their marriage is alien to the teaching of Islam, though it must happen in exceptional cases.

Muhammed himself was not at all prudish about sex. The Prophet was prepared to answer intimate questions, and frequently gave advice with disarming and commendable directness. His recorded utterances cover everything from menstruation to impotency. He maintained that both partners have a duty to love, honour, and satisfy the needs of their spouses, and that only by following this rule can a marriage be preserved without suffering, guilt, and depression. Mohammed urged men to respect their wives, to consider their needs, and to cherish them. Al-Ghazzali reported Muhammad as saying that a man should not satisfy his need of his wife until he had satisfied her need of him.

This is all well and good, but there are other things Muhammad is recorded to have said that inspire a raised eyebrow, if not a sense of horror, in any non-Muslim. If wives or husbands refused each other's advances, the Prophet apparently said, 'The angels would curse them until morning.' At other times he said, 'By Him in whose hand is my life, when a man calls his wife to his bed and she does not respond, the One in heaven is displeased with her until her husband is pleased with her'. Another *hadith* says, 'The woman who sleeps elsewhere than in her husband's bed is accursed by the angels until she returns to it.' Yet another states that a woman must never refuse her husband 'even when busy at the oven'; another even when she is riding a camel. Muslims argue that statements such as these should be read in the wider context: a woman should respond to her husband's needs no matter how much she has to do because this protects the chastity of a marriage and prevents him looking elsewhere.

The different attitudes to sex held by Islamic societies and secular ones have been further highlighted by history. The non-Muslim view of sex has been revolutionised by two world wars, the decline of the influence of the Church, and by the advent of easy and safe contraception. There is a widespread opinion, in many Muslim societies, that the West is immoral to its core. Many non-Muslims believe that personal morality demands respect and concern for the other person in a relationship, and that, provided there is mutual consent about bedroom behaviour, it is moral. This does reflect the Muslim attitude (that what a married couple do behind closed doors is their own affair), but it has also resulted in the acceptance of what could be called serial monogamy before marriage. Modern nightclub culture and the concomitant one-night stands have upset the sexual norms of the previous forty years. The club scene, in general, with its deliberate drunkenness and the expectation of casual sexual encounters, is offensive to those who have been brought up within the Muslim faith. A non-Muslim's experience of Muslims is sometimes limited to seeing the occasional 'possibly Muslim' man in a bar or club, or perhaps even to brief liaisons with young Muslim men. It leads them to the conclusion that the Muslims sexual code is more honoured in theory than in practice; but this ignores the great loyalty a Muslim husband shows to his family.

In all religions and cultures, there are those who choose to be celibate. They feel that they are married to God. In the secular West, the wisdom or appeal of this may be doubted, but in general it is accepted as a valid reason for celibacy – and, indeed there are no shortage of Westerners who, for religious or personal reasons, choose not to engage in sexual practices. Christians are brought up to believe that Jesus was celibate throughout his life, and that the Virgin Mary conceived him without an earthly sexual encounter. Buddhist monks are celibate, with some exceptions among the Japanese. Some Hindu men (called *sannyasin*) in the fourth and final stage of life leave the comfort of their house, and the pleasures of their wives, to achieve liberation and communion with God. They are living the same feelings and aspirations as St Etheldreda of Ely, who abandoned domesticity and remained a virgin in order to found a great church for the glory of God.

Interestingly, Muslims regard sexual abstinence with a certain degree of suspicion, and even bafflement. Celibacy is often seen not as a sign of devotion, but as a form of ingratitude towards Allah. To deny one's natural urges, as Christianity so often demands, goes against one of the basic tenets of the Islamic faith. It is as unpraiseworthy for followers of Islam to fail to fulfill their sexual potential as it was for the man in the Biblical parable to bury his talent. Islam, therefore, does not hold that a celibate life is a holier life: abstinence from other things may not be alien to Muslims, but refraining from sex is not recognised as a means to God. Some Muslims like to pray before sex. To us this may seem as outdated as saying grace before dinner, but some of our great-grandparents may well have done the same. And as Catholics have a reputation for, somewhat comically, leaping out of bed after the act for a shower, so too Muslims often perform ritual purification after sex. The mistake is to believe that these rituals are laid down because sex is regarded as somehow improper, indecent or wrong. They are not.

A belief in the traditional value of virginity before marriage is fundamental to Islam: there are overwhelming social pressures on Middle Eastern women to be unspoilt before they marry. But this creates problems. In her book *Women and Sex*, Nawal al-Saadawi, the great Egyptian writer and physician, suggests that the suppression of an adolescent girl's burgeoning sexual impulses may have lasting ill effects. In her opinion, it is unrealistic to expect a woman to blossom sexually on her wedding night (it is highly unlikely that her husband will have denied himself until then). 'Many Muslim women,' she adds, 'may not even realise that they are supposed to enjoy sex in marriage because they are often brought up to think of sex purely as a duty to their husband.'

As to exactly what constitutes sex to a Muslim, this is as impossible a question to answer as what constitutes sex to a Briton; however, it is true that oral and anal sex have been used by both sexes to circumvent the hymeneal pre-requisite. Sex while a woman is menstruating (and is therefore unclean) is forbidden. Masturbation is frowned on, but tolerated, particularly by the Hanbali school, which acknowledges the inevitability of its occurrence and recognises the need for single males to release tension. Masturbation is also seen as a means by which the impulse to fornicate or commit adultery is dissipated. Strict Muslims, who believe in legal penalties for sex outside of marriage, have their own views on the subject.

To many people, one of the more unsavoury aspects of Western sexual relationships today is the lack of discretion that one or other partner may display about revealing its physical details. Recently it has become commonplace to hear people discussing the secrets of their sex life. The Qur'an deals robustly with this lack of consideration for another person's privacy, dictating that marital relationships should be kept discreet. The intimate details of the marriage and the bedroom should never be divulged, nor discussed with outsiders. Likewise, public displays of affection are generally forbidden in Islam, as they are in Western corporate culture. Given that Islam encourages sex as healthy and normal, it is easier to understand why there are so many proscriptions when it comes to avoiding temptation – for example, unmarried men and women are discouraged from being alone together.

At the heart of these guidelines are decency and modesty. In strict Muslim countries, including Iran and Saudi Arabia, illicit public sexual behaviour, or *zina*, is a punishable offence. Of course, in other parts of the Muslim world, the rules are not so strict: in Egypt there is a cultural ritual, known as the *basbasa*, in which a woman will pass by men in the street, swinging her hips. The manner in which she wears her veil, the tinkling of her jewellery, and the scent she leaves behind, signal that she is available. Men stare, and sometimes shout obscenities. The woman then slows down her walk, dragging her feet. It is a form of veiled (in both senses) emotional striptease. *Basbasa* is sometimes also practised within groups of women.

Young people in many parts of the Middle East maintain secret relationships before marriage to someone else. These may continue for a long time, sometimes years, even though there is no possibility of physical contact. Today, these forbidden friendships, previously pursued by furtive glances and *billets-doux*, may be reliant on mobile telephones. Both parties may experience illicit and essentially innocent pleasure, but both are always careful not to be discovered.

Although the rich tradition of erotic Arab literature may suggest a culture obsessed with sex, promiscuity was and still is regarded as a grave abuse of Allah's intentions. Significantly, Satan is depicted in the Qur'an as a seducer, 'the insidious tempter who whispers in the hearts of men'. If a Muslim is pressed about what does and does not constitute promiscuity, the response varies enormously, depending upon where in the Muslim world he lives. The line between rampant polygamy and unbridled promiscuity does not seem to be sharply defined.

Prostitution is banned, but still common, throughout most of the Muslim world. Before the advent of Islam, it was more obvious and widespread, but despite Muhammad's condemnation of it, prostitution continues, as it does everywhere else in the world. There is not a single Muslim town of any importance that does not have a brothel. Sometimes, as in Beirut, or Kairwan, they are to be found at some distance from the city centre. In other countries, such as in Tunisia, the red-light area is, as in Amsterdam or London, in the very heart of the city. Prostitutes, especially in small towns, are often known by name, and not necessarily shunned. Some are even thought of as professionals, and occasionally may be invited to family celebrations to amuse the guests with their racy talk. Once married, despite initial objections, they can become integrated into the life of the community. Although the prostitute is an outsider, she has a recognised role to play in the community. Prostitution has, arguably, become institutionalised in many Muslim countries. Prostitutes are called upon to initiate adolescent men into the world of sex, and generations of males claim to have benefited from this.

A more contentious issue is that of homosexuality, which is totally forbidden anywhere in the Muslim world, and abhorrent to Muslims. It is regarded by some unequivocally as a grave sin; but for many Muslims being gay is seen as a test, a problem to be overcome, and not a fault of their making. It is something to be coped with because it is forbidden in the Qur'an, and in a revelation to Moses concerning the story of Lot and the people of Sodom. Mohammad stressed that there were differences between men and women, and that these should be preserved. Those who follow Prophet encourage the outward and visible signs of gender differences, which range from the beard, symbol of virility, to the veil, a sign of feminine humility. Homosexuality is regarded as an aberration that contradicts the natural order.

There is no shortage of scriptural prohibitions against homosexuality in any of the Judaeo-Christian texts. Muslims who argue vehemently against homosexuality quote Muhammad's words: 'Will you approach males and abandon those whom God created for you as mates?' They assert that sex between people of the same gender was forbidden by Allah in a revelation to the Prophet; they recount the story of Lot; and Allah's words to the people of Sodom: 'You satisfy your lust with men instead of women. Indeed you are a nation that has transgressed beyond bounds.' The nature versus nurture arguments are of no import in Islam. Nothing is an excuse for giving in to perverse and deviant sexual desires. To be homosexual is regarded as an impediment, a disability, and even a curse.

Attitudes to homosexuality in the Western secular societies have softened only recently, with homosexuals being allowed to marry in some places, and raise children, but condemnation of it by Muslims is no less round than it was centuries ago. The Muslim cleric Dr Yusuf al-Qaradawi has, on a number of occasions, decreed homosexuality to be 'an unnatural and evil practice'. In his book, *The Lawful and Prohibited in Islam*, the adjectives he uses to describe lesbian and gay people include 'perverted', 'shameless', 'aberrant', 'unnatural', 'foul', and 'illicit'.

It is argued that the segregation of the sexes in Islamic society throughout the ages has served to encourage the development of homosexuality. Historically, in European literature, few gay poets have openly paraded their passions and many gay writers, painters, and musicians have stayed quiet about their inclinations, whereas Islamic poets often sang of their love of adolescent boys. The sexual instincts were readily aroused by the constant spectacle of so many beautiful naked bodies displayed in the public baths – a sexually charged experience. But neither the religious nor the social conscience of Islam could put an end to undesirable practices, however much they might be despised. Society turned a blind eye to those practices that it could not eliminate. These ranged from pederasty to lesbianism, both of which may well have been partly consequences of the strict separation of the sexes.

CHAPTER 15

The second sex

Women undoubtedly have an important role to play within the family unit under Islam, both as wives and mothers, but one of the most controversial issues preventing lasting harmony, if not integration, between Muslim and non-Muslim is the status of women within society. In some Islamic countries, women are not allowed to travel far afield, meet a man, or take part in various activities, without the permission of the male head of the house, whether father, husband, or brother. This may seem strange to non-Muslims, but their parents' generation will doubtless remember how, in childhood, they were expected to seek their fathers' approval before they did anything of import. Even now, we could hardly say that the mantra 'Ask your father,' has completely disappeared. Perhaps before non-Muslims attack Islam for being patriarchal, sexist, and cruel, they should consider that the secular West has only really moved on in the past seventy years. Even after the Second World War, which was a catalyst to the sexual revolution, it was still common for politicians when canvassing to ask women how their husbands would be expecting them to vote. It was generally felt that men were more competent to make major decisions than women, although the women's interests and opinions would have been considered. Is religion to blame for what many see as the unfair treatment and low social status of Muslim women in our modern age, or are cultural practices that have predominated for centuries?

In order to unravel the question, Muslim scholars refer us initially to the context of society during Muhammad's lifetime, when the social status of woman in Arab society – as in the West – was exceedingly low. Despite the elaborate rhapsodies to women in the songs and music of the Arabian lands at this time, the adoration of women was more inspired by carnal lust and feelings of ownership than by a true understanding of their potential, their dignity, or their humanity. Women at that time were often accorded treatment little better than that lavished upon a favourite horse. Prostitution was a recognised profession: captive women, kept as handmaids, were forced to make money for their masters, who were also their pimps. Husbands were more interested in the continuation of the family than having the exclusive sexual rights to their wives. Married women who had not conceived were allowed by their husbands to have sex with others so as to improve their chances of becoming pregnant, a practice known in the Islamic world as *istibdza*, which was also known to operate at one time or another in many other societies.

Women in the days before the Prophet Muhammad were treated as chattels. A woman was not entitled to inherit any share of the estate of her deceased husband, father, or other relation. On the contrary, she herself was inherited as part of the property. The man who inherited her could, if he wished, marry her, but he might instead choose to lend or give her to someone else. On the death of his father, a son could even marry his stepmother. Like the sheep, camels, and carpets, she was part of his inheritance. A man could repeatedly divorce his wife, then take her back again, provided it was within a prescribed period known as *'iddah*. He could swear never to have sexual relations with the spurned woman again, but resume relations if the mood took him. He could declare that henceforth he would look upon her 'as his mother', so that for an unspecified time she had little idea of her future role. A woman's life was devoid of security.

The revolution of Arab society heralded by the advent of Islam and the teachings of the Prophet brought about a change in the status of women. Qur'anic injunctions against the abuse of women, and the provisions made in Islam for their protection, did for women what the Magna Carta in England did for government. The Qur'an gave women rights of inheritance and divorce, centuries before Western women were accorded similar benefits. It did not, however, effect immediate or revolutionary change, nor has it ever created equity in women's rights. Even now, women suffer restrictions in some Islamic countries that would never be tolerated in the West.

Muhammad taught men that the best among them was he who treated his wife best. To plant respect and regard for women in a soil where infants of that sex were frequently buried alive was no easy task: the birth of a daughter was no occasion for celebration in pre-Islamic

Arabia (nor, some would argue, even now). Before Islam, the daughter would often have been disposed of to save her father's face; it was a mark of virility and power to father sons. Women generally had little say in the fate of their daughters – it was their failure, too – and sometimes explicit agreement was given at the nuptial ceremony to the slaughter of female children. There were cases in which the agreement went beyond this, and decreed it would be the duty of the mother herself to perform the infanticide. Such brutal practices came to an end at a single stroke, with the Qur'anic words, 'And when the one buried alive is asked for what sin she was killed . . .' If Muslims' interpretation of, and obedience to, the Qur'an has so far failed to accord the women even the status accorded to them by the Prophet, it has at least succeeded in outlawing the live burial of female children. Once Islam became firmly established, there were no further recorded instances of this cruelty.

If the good that Muhammad achieved for women is weighed against the failure of Islam to achieve equality for them 1,400 years later, there can be little doubt that his influence was regarded as wholly positive. The number of wives Muhammad had has been held against him by non-Muslims, but this reflected the custom of his own lands in the times in which he lived. There is much evidence that Muhammad was a loyal and devoted family man. For many years, he remained monogamous, which was unusual in an Arabian country. Khadija bore him four daughters, all of whom he treated with kindness and humanity. Muslims maintain that Muhammad was a man who truly enjoyed the company of women, and tradition holds that some of his male companions were astonished by his leniency towards his wives. They were amazed at the way in which he allowed them to stand up to him. He was scrupulous about helping with the chores, and even mended his own clothes. Whenever he had the opportunity, he sought out the companionship and counsel of his wives. Not only would he take them on expeditions, but he would take their advice seriously. Where their education was concerned, tradition holds that all the women in Medina were taught by Muhammad, and that during his lifetime men were also being taught by knowledgeable and respected women, Umm Darda, Shifa bint Abdullah, Umm Waraqah, and Aisha among them.

Critics of Islam argue that the Qur'an does appear to suggest the primacy of man over woman. Woman proceeds from man; she is chronologically secondary. She finds her fulfillment through man. She is made for his pleasure, his repose, and his fulfilment. This primacy of the male seems to be exemplified by a much-debated verse, *surah* 2:28, which is often translated as 'Husbands have a degree [of right] over them [their wives].' Muslims argue that the context of this statement relates to the question of rights of divorce between husbands and wives. Partly because of a misinterpretation of this verse, they say, very strict Muslims subsequently prohibited the appointment of female judges. Other Muslim scholars of the nineteenth and twentieth centuries have similarly used *hadith*s from the collections of Bukhari and Abu Muslim to support the argument that women are intrinsically inferior to men. One scholar, Riffat Hassan, has examined these claims in detail, and maintains all these *hadith*s can be traced to a

contemporary companion of Muhammad called Abu
Hurairah. Such *hadith*s are most commonly dismissed as
unreliable, he says, and do not reflect the sayings or beliefs
of the Prophet. They simply reflect prejudices that existed
in early Islamic culture.

Another verse that has been interpreted as justifying the
disregard of women under Islam is 2:282. This has often
been translated into English to read 'Call in two men as
witnesses. If two men are not there, then call one man and
two women out of those you approve as witnesses, so that
if one of the two women should err the other can remind
her.' In this instance, Muslims stress that the translation of
the original Arabic *tadilla* as 'err' is not correct, and that the
verb has many other meanings, including 'forget'. The
correct translation should be, they say: 'If one of the two
women should forget, the other can remind her.' This, they
declare, puts an altogether different – and much less
derogatory – slant on the verse, whose point is about
protecting people's property. When Muhammad received
his revelation on the subject, women were less involved in
financial matters than men were, and less literate. It has to
be understood in the different cultural context.

Muslims stress that, in fact, the Qur'an makes women
and men equal partners before God. They are not inferior,
but created from the same soul. However, each of the sexes
has differing duties and responsibilities. Every instruction
given to Muslims in the Qur'an refers to male and female
believers alike. Both sexes are judged by the same
standards, and both have the same religious obligations.
One *hadith* tells how the Prophet's wife Salamah asked
God one day why the Qur'an's revelations never specifi-

cally mentioned women. He replied by stressing the equality of both. In the Arabic, the word *insan* refers not just to men, as some people have maintained, but to both sexes. 'For men and women who are patient and constant, who humble themselves, who give in charity, who fast, who guard their chastity, and who engage in the praise of Allah . . . Allah has prepared forgiveness and a great reward.'

That men and women have different roles according to Islam is exemplified by the Islamic view of a married couple, a view based on complementary harmony of the sexes, and where the dichotomy of the sexes is carefully marked out before God. Man and woman are different, and the ideal state is a union of the two. A harmonious union can only be achieved if the qualities both bring to the marriage are complementary to one another. In Islam, this principle, established first in a household, applies equally outside it. Unity and harmony in the world can only be achieved if there is harmony between the sexes, and the best way of realising that harmony is for a man to be masculine and for a woman to be feminine. There should be no guilt or denial about the differences between the sexes: these are, in fact, the very things that make them available and desirable to one another. Such a dialogue between the sexes should be carried out in an atmosphere of mutual respect. The division of labour between men and women has been codified in Islamic law, and in many ways it might be argued that it favours the lot of the woman in that the man has to keep her and protect her. Inheritance laws in Islamic countries take into account the financial responsibilities men have to their family, and where men receive larger shares of an estate, it is because they are expected to provide for women, whereas women's shares are theirs to keep.

It appears to many non-Muslims that some Muslim countries have taken this essential difference between the role of man and women in society to extremes. Although a Muslim husband must take good care of his wife, be financially generous with her, and do his best to treat her fairly, he does not necessarily regard her as being capable of performing certain tasks. Although it is apparently contradictory to the dictates of Islam, women are none the less forbidden in some Islamic countries to drive. They certainly not allowed to have their own circle of male friends. As in Britain, the jobs open to many Muslim women in the Middle East are as limited as they were to British women only sixty or seventy years ago. If women in Muslim countries do go out to work, the job must be compatible with the teachings of the Qur'an.

Down the centuries, changes in the pattern of women's working are complex, varying from country to country, depending on many factors, such as opportunity, literacy, and poverty. Nowadays, in some areas of the Middle East, if a Muslim daughter survives infancy she is made to work as soon as she is able. The sight of young girls working in a run-down part of a town, or in a poverty-stricken country district is a common one. Small girls labouring, or caring for younger siblings, may often be seen trying to find a few moments to play games in a day devoted to working. Their mothers, preoccupied with continual pregnancies, charge their small daughters with duties ranging from fetching water to keeping the house clean, expecting them from an early age act as unpaid helpers. In Afghanistan, in the strictest Islamic areas, women still receive very little education that would allow them to secure improved job opportunities, whereas in other parts of the Islamic world, although educated separately from men, quite often at university level, women follow academic and business careers. In the strict Islamic world, once married it is very unlikely that a woman would continue to work, while in other countries married women have risen to the top of their professions. It is impossible to generalise. In Saudi Arabia, only five per cent of the workforce is female, but in Egypt juggling a profession and marriage is common.

To what extent Islam is responsible for this is highly arguable. The Qur'an is all-important, and is at the heart of all decisions taken, but the way in which its verses are interpreted varies. Arguably it has more to do with cultural practices and attitudes. Muslim scholars stress there is no rule in Islam against women working, assuming that the work involved is compatible with the tenets of the religion. Indeed, Islamic society needs Muslim women to work, for example, as doctors, nurses, and lawyers treating and advising other women. Comparisons in non-Muslim, secular society are hard to find, although in early-twentieth-century England, in households that were financially secure, there was no pressure on women to work, because it was accepted that a woman, once married, had the right to expect to be kept by her husband. In less fortunate houses, whether in the East or West, circumstances often forced women to work in order that the family might have adequate funds. At the other end of the social scale, in both East and West, some women, although well-off, choose to pursue a career. The Prophet's wife Khadija was, as we have seen, a successful businesswoman, and had been the Prophet's employer before she became his wife; several of his later wives also earned their own incomes.

Since men and women have different roles in society, does this mean they have to live separately? To be a Muslim woman in some countries is to live incognito. Even the Arab house becomes a sort of veil. Most mosques have separate entrances for men and women, and women pray in a separate area. Muslim men are expected to take a leader's role in public, as a woman does in the home. In public, women often appear shy, and reluctant to speak with strangers. Many welcome the privacy and anonymity that the *hijab* (veil) offers, and many are even pleased to shelter behind the all-covering *chador* that in some parts of the world leaves only their eyes visible.

Opinions regarding the seclusion of women vary widely. Conservative Muslims often say women should not only remain secluded in the house, but that they should go out only with their husbands or other male family members; and that if they go to work or to school, the sexes there should be segregated. In many Muslim countries, this remains the case. But it is important to remember that such decisions are influenced by local custom and culture. In Saudi Arabia, there is a shopping mall just for women; in Kabul, a market just for women. Throughout the Middle East, many schools still echo the original pattern of British state education by dividing boys from girls. As part of the protection afforded women, Islam teaches that women should not be forced by men to go out and earn money. The Prophet was alert to the injustices that could be inflicted on working women, and a *hadith* by Abu Muslim that states: 'Allah will definitely enforce the settlement of the dues of those entitled to receive them on the day of judgement; even the wrong done to the hornless goat [i.e. the female] by the horned goat [i.e. the male] will be redressed.'

Muslim scholars stress that the widespread seclusion or segregation of Muslim women is not an Islamic dictate: it was never actually instructed by the Prophet. The Qur'an itself prescribes some degree of segregation for the wives, but there is nothing in it that requires their total seclusion in a separate part of the house. Such customs were adopted some three or four generations after the Prophet's death. Originally, the seclusion of women was an ancient cultural practice adopted as far back as the third century by the wealthier classes who wished to preserve their privacy. Scholars say that the practice of total seclusion in Islamic society probably arose from a disputed interpretation of the verses in the Qur'an that were addressed to the Prophet's wives, in particular *surah* 33.32–3: 'O wives of the Prophet! You are not like ordinary women. If you fear Allah, don't be too casual in your speech, lest someone with an unsteadfast heart should be moved with desire . . . live quietly in your houses and don't make a worldly display, as in the times of ignorance; establish regular prayer and give regular charity, and obey Allah and his apostle.'

Strict orthodox Muslims have interpreted this to mean women should always remain in their homes; if they wish to do so, it is their prerogative, but they should not be actively forced to do so. Muhammad's wives circulated freely, retreating to their houses for privacy when appropriate. They and the women of Medina went with the men to pray together at the mosque, took a full part in public life, and even, according to Arab tradition, sometimes fought alongside men in battle.

CHAPTER 16

Guarding their modesty

Whatever its degree of coverage, the veil has always been an iconic symbol of all Muslim women, whether mothers, wives or daughters, and whatever their place in society. Because covering up is such an everyday and ordinary part of life for their part, Muslims are, understandably, often surprised by objections to it. For many, the veil is a badge of honour and a sign of their devotion to and love for God. For many non-Muslims, however, when worn by Muslim women living in secular Western societies, it remains an object of mistrust, and a symbol of division.

Scholars debate the origin of veiling, all agreeing that it lies in pre-Islamic history, and that the precise details of its origin have been lost. It is claimed by some advocates of the veil that the rules governing its use were initially proposed by Caliph Omar I. Omar was proud that it was God Himself who had handed His instructions to him. Most scholars hold that the covering of the head is not only an Islamic tradition, but one that existed among Arabian camel-herders and Persians in the Fertile Crescent before Islam. In the hot desert climates of Arabia and

Jordan, as in Saudi Arabia, the wearing of a head rope over a traditional headscarf indicated tribal identity in the greater tribal groups, such as of the Mintifij and the Bani Huchaim. A head covering performed a cultural role. It distinguished the origins of the wearer, and was determined by custom rather than Islamic law.

As with other head coverings, the veil was not confined to Muslim women, but was common among many peoples in the eastern Mediterranean at the time of Muhammad. It was a practice that had been adopted by Greek women as far back as the third century, long before the life of the Prophet. It had formed part of the dress code of some upper-class Hindu sects, Persians, and even some Christians. Women from prosperous families, who lived a secluded life, wore a veil as a physical representation of their social separation; and in turn the veil became a sign of an upwardly mobile family, since only the urban rich and wealthy merchant families could afford to spare women the burden of manual work. In the early days of Islam, as the number of slaves and concubines began to increase – with the result that the practice of seclusion became common throughout Muslim society – the social significance of veiling decreased.

Veiling was originally a personal choice, a matter for a family to decide themselves, but many women chose to follow in the footsteps of the path laid down by the Prophet's wives. A veiled woman was once something of great value to a man: veiled women of the upper classes were kept as slaves in large female courts, or *harems*, in the households of the elite ruling classes. In the *harem* culture, which continued to develop throughout the Middle Ages, for example, during the Mamluk period in Egypt, veiling made a statement about ownership as well as class.

It was only later that the veil came to represent the Islamic male concern for preserving the chastity of a woman. Some men, often fathers, feared this chastity might be endangered, and with its loss, the family honour besmirched, if a woman of the family was seen by other men. The association of the veil with chastity was such that many Muslim men came to fear contact with unveiled women. Conservative Muslim theologians regarded a woman without a veil as guilty of attempting to seduce every man she came into contact with; but this might suggest more about a man's lack of control than a woman's desire to corrupt him.

Neither the Qur'an nor the *hadiths* contain clear, specific instructions ordering that women should be veiled; nowhere does the Qur'an explicitly require that all women should cover up. Verse 33:53 of the Qur'an is the most quoted on the subject, but this was intended specifically for Muhammad's wives. It does refer to a veil or *hijab*, but that is almost universally understood to denote a curtain in their homes rather than an item of clothing. 'And when you ask something from the Prophet's wives, do so from behind a *hijab*. This will ensure the purity of your hearts as well as theirs.'

The verse that most Muslims refer to on the subject of veiling is 24:30-31: 'Believing women should lower their gaze and guard their modesty. They should not display their ornaments, except as is normal. They should draw their veils over their bosoms and not display their beauty unless to their close relatives.' God's instruction is for women to cover their bosoms. It contains the implication that they are already wearing a veil. Yet some Muslim women have interpreted the verse to mean they should cover their curves rather than their heads.

Undoubtedly they were prohibited from showing any cleavage, and had to cover any provocative garments with an outer layer when in public and under no circumstances breast-feed in public. Debate still rages among Muslims regarding the precise meaning of 'ornaments'. Some say it relates to expensive jewellery; others jump to the other extreme, claiming it means a woman's voice, even. In some quarters it means the covering of the full face (although in many *hadith*s womens' faces are visible). Some very strict Muslims have suggested that make-up even, because it masks the true face of a woman, is a form of veil. This seems ironic, given that the point of make-up is to attract attention. Others have extended that argument by suggesting that the wearing of provocative clothing draws attention to a woman's femininity, so that their sexuality is accentuated to the point at which it hides their true personality. In more Westernised parts of the Middle East, such as in Egypt, the Lebanon and Jordan, make-up is commonly worn for all to see.

If the Qur'an is ambiguous on the subject of veiling, the *hadith*s, without specifically making an injunction, indicate clearly that Muhammad had asked his wives to wear a veil. Nothing of a female, he said, past the age of puberty should be seen except the hands or face. This had helped his wives to separate themselves from the crowds who milled around the Prophet's house. History records that Aisha, wife of the Prophet Muhammad, felt able to attend a mosque only because she was adequately veiled, and therefore could sit near men.

Veiling nowadays is a complex issue. The modern Islamic world is by no means a homogeneous mass with respect to clothing, nor indeed to anything else. In some areas women have always been expected to cover up completely. Here, a full-face veil has always been considered essential, or at least a garment that leaves only the eyes visible. In other countries, and at different times, covering of the lower face has been all that is expected. In a few places, covering the hair is adequate; this is the path many Muslim women living in the West today, and some in Muslim countries, consider sufficient. Regional variations, where they exist, are usually determined by local custom and culture, not by religious differences. A veil worn by a Lebanese or Saudi woman is quite different from that worn by an Iranian.

Over the centuries, not only the styles of veils and other head coverings have varied, but also the words used to describe them have differed according to regional custom and language. The *hijab* is a head covering, and is the most commonly seen item in and out of the Muslim world. In Iran and South Asia, a garment known as a *chador* covers the entire body from head to foot. The only part of the body that is exposed is the eyes, to allow the woman to see. The *abaya* in Saudia Arabia and the *burqa* in Pakistan and Afghanistan are also loose garments that envelop the entire head and body. The *khimar* is a head-and-shoulders piece, worn throughout the Middle East, which extends down to the chest. It may be worn with the *hibab*, which covers the rest of the body.

The Muslim rationale for wearing modest clothing is that it is unfair to men, who ought not to be subjected to temptations their religion does not allow them to pursue. To achieve this, women must conceal the outline of their body. Blouses will invariably be long-sleeved, and neither flesh nor underclothing should be visible through the blouse, which should be loose enough that it does not emphasise the shape of the breasts. If a woman wears *shalwar khameez*, a tunic that covers the top of the trousers, the trousers must be baggy so as not to accentuate her figure. In strict Muslim societies there are precise rules about what parts of the body should be seen only by partners in the matrimonial bedroom. Skimpy or transparent clothing is to be avoided. In the most austere Muslim households, women reveal only their face and hands, though this is more unusual. Unless a Muslim woman is wearing the full *burqa*, she is free to experiment with her clothing within the bounds of decency and good taste. Many Muslim women choose to cover their hair, as the hair is seen as a symbol of female sexuality. In many countries, this seems mandatory – but, again, it is not a religious requirement.

The general rule of modesty is a simple one, and is the only one given in the Qu'ran. While remaining within culturally defined conventions, women in Muslim countries have more scope than is generally realised to celebrate their individuality. That said, they are neither allowed to, nor would want to, flaunt their sexuality in public nor emphasise their femininity. This is in stark contrast to the fashions that dominate the West, where clothes are designed to accentuate a person's physical assets, and where Sartre spoke of the confrontation of the sexes as an *être-regard*, 'being as a look'. To be a Muslim is to act modestly in all respects, to control one's gaze, and to know how to protect one's privacy from others.

Dress beneath the veil is largely a cultural matter. Although the outer layer of clothing worn by Muslim women is usually sober, black in most parts of the Islamic world and blue in some others, the inner clothing may be brightly coloured. It may vary from the bright Chanel suits sported by rich women in Tehran – hidden beneath their religious garments – to the strong primary colours traditionally worn by Muslims living in the heart of the Arabian peninsula. In some parts of Saudi Arabia, muted greys, blues, greens, or beiges are popular. In Islamic countries, as in the rest of the world, older women argue it is more respectable for them to wear subdued colours with delicate patterns. It is only Bedouins, they scoff, who wear loud colours with bold patterns. Such observations, of course, have nothing to do with Islam: these are societal attitudes and cultural traditions.

With such differences of interpretation in the scriptures, it is hardly surprising that veiling has become highly contentious. In some countries, choosing to wear, or not to wear, it has become a political issue. A *burqa* that reveals only a woman's eyes has caused not only surprise, but true offence, both to non-Muslims and to Muslims who do not see the need for it. It is interpreted by non-Muslims as a desire to remain separate from the non-Muslim community, and to reject any notion of integration. Others regard the veil in much the same way as national football supporters regard an opponent's flag: as a passionate statement of identity and commitment to faith, the importance of which over-rides any deference to the country where the wearer is living, and in which she may have been born.

What is more, women who freely choose to wear it are often derided as weak and oppressed. In the late nineteenth century another ironic development arose. Apparently endangered by an excessive and decadent Western culture, and occasional Western Islamophobia, Muslims ascribed a new significance to the *hijab* as it became a symbol of the resistance to Western influence. Failing to wear it was a sign of opposition to the patriarchal system that had controlled Islamic society for centuries, and perhaps a sign of the endorsement of Western values.

Among the first Muslim rulers who tried to Westernise their countries by abandoning the veil were Kemal Atatürk, who abolished the caliphate in Turkey and attempted to turn the country into a modern secular state, and Qassim Amin, leader of Egypt. Led by Huda al-Sha'rawi in 1923, Egyptian women stopped their tradition of veil-wearing. This stimulated a violent reaction; a conservative response to defend and uphold Islamic teachings, traditions, and lifestyle. Heated debate amongst Muslims resulted in the veil being reasserted as a traditional symbol of the exclusive and respected sexual and familial role of women. In Turkey, the majority of the educated classes followed the leadership of Atatürk, abandoned the veil, and became, to all intents and purposes, Westernised. In recent years, however, there has been a resurgence of veiling, and of strict obedience to Islamic teaching, which has produced political and civil discord. In France, where the veil has recently been banned in public, feminists and strict Muslim women have united over their right to wear it.

Many Muslim women argue that, in fact, it takes tremendous courage to wear the *hijab* in a non-Muslim country, and that this expression of belief has nothing to do with pressure from their husbands or families, but is a personal choice, a reflection of their love of God, and something to be proud of. Marginalised by racial and religious intolerance, many women, retreating into the comfort of their faith, paradoxically perform such acts of courage – like leaving the house in a *burqa* – thus potentially exposing themselves to ridicule or abuse. It is a great irony in such instances that to many non-Muslims it continues to represent oppression.

Men are also controlled by cultural considerations when choosing their clothes. One set of *hadiths*, those of Bukhari, include an entire book devoted to the correct style of dress for both men and women. The Muslim man must always dress modestly, covering himself from the navel to the knees. He must respect the over-riding principle that everything he wears defines his gender and differentiates his appearance from that of a woman. Any attempt by women to look like a man by dressing in male clothing is disapproved of by the Prophet and strictly forbidden. Any man who wears overtly feminine clothing is equally condemned.

Muslims of course understand that clothes must be practical: they are not only worn to uphold or express religious beliefs. But any garment that a Muslim man wears should not accentuate his sexuality: a generously cut shirt and loose-fitting trousers are the norm. Islamic clothing attempts to obscure the outline of male and female bodies so as to avoid their being provocative. The Prophet also warned that men should be careful when undressing in public, so they do not unintentionally display their nakedness.

Two small idiosyncrasies of male dress continue to be respected in many areas. The first is that men should wear cotton rather than silk. There is a *hadith*, according to Abu Daoud that reports: 'It has been forbidden for the males of any nation to wear silk and gold[,] which is [only] allowed for females.' Traditionally, silk was made for women. The second is the notion that gold jewellery is forbidden for men. In some areas this is not regarded as necessary. One of the reasons that wealthy Arabs can often be seen with expensive gold wristwatches is that it is one of the few adornments that they can acceptably sport in public.

CHAPTER 17

Eat only the good things

However contentious the dress and role of Muslim women in society as a whole, many who are homemakers and who receive guests into their home pride themselves on the preparation of food according to the Islamic principles taught by Muhammad, as laid down in the Qur'an. Although what is eaten naturally varies according to region and culture – for example, Bosnian Muslims are unlikely to share the rich and colourful palate of their wealthier brothers in Saudi Arabia – there are universal practices common to most Muslims regarding food, according to religious principles.

The rules of purity and cleanliness in Islam involve all parts of the body and spirit, so it is not surprising that Muslims are meticulous and ingenious about cooking and eating. Muslims seek to free themselves of spiritual and physical impurity in order to become closer to God, not just through fasting, and washing before prayer, but also in what they take into their bodies. It follows logically that if possible the containers in which food is stored or prepared in the Islamic kitchen are spotless. The pots and pans all smell clean and fresh, and the people sitting down to any meal are well washed. Only when clean are guests considered ready to enjoy the food that has been equally carefully prepared.

Muslims follow strict guidelines as to what kind of animal meat should or should not be eaten. All food is either *halal* (allowed) or *haram* (forbidden). Following the rules as given by God to Muhammad is regarded as discipline and submission to the will of God by all Muslims today, just as it was when Muhammad was alive. 'O believers! Eat of the good things that we have provided for you, and be grateful to God if it is Him you worship.' The two verses in the Qur'an containing the instruction, *surah* 2:172, and *surah* 5:4, specify clearly what Muslims can and cannot eat. Broadly speaking, all food is *halal*, except for meat from swine, or its by-products, from animals improperly slaughtered, animals killed in the name of anyone but God, intoxicants, blood and blood by-products, or foods contaminated with any of these things.

Halal slaughter requires that animals should bleed to death, a method that causes great controversy in the non-Muslim world. Only those parts of the animal unlikely to have been contaminated, either before or during slaughter, are eaten. Meat is bled and then washed. The knives, vessels and surfaces are washed. Although all these measures are incorporated into Islamic law, they could equally well be the standards of any non-Muslim public-health expert working in a hot climate.

Following God's prohibition on eating pork today, any part of the pig is still considered abhorrent on account of its impurity, and because it is a breeding ground of bacteria and a cause of disease. Muslims say the pig is banned because it eats its own excrement, and in some places it is deliberately encouraged to do so. Pork still rouses such strong feelings of revulsion that anything touched by a pig is considered contaminated, and therefore worthless.

Some scholars point out a pragmatic, historical root to the practice: pork cannot be eaten once it has gone off, unlike beef, which can be safely ingested some time after it has started to turn. In the hot climates that make up much of the Muslim world, flesh goes off very quickly, and meat that could not be stored would have been considered useless. It is easy to imagine how those who were, through poverty, forced to risk it – and who then became ill as a result – branded the animal responsible as either unclean or diseased.

Avoidance of all pork is a practice that sharply distinguishes Muslims from Christians; Jews also refrain from eating it. As a result of the prohibition in the Qur'an from the seventh century onwards, Islamic countries have been essentially pig-less. Pigs have had a bad press even beyond Muslim society. They are subject to a large number of jibes and derisory references in literature and language – 'to make a pig's ear' of something means to handle it ineptly; 'to make a pig of oneself' means to eat copiously; to 'squeal like a pig' or 'sweat like a pig'.

Non-Muslims, though, generally see them very differently. The view that pigs are filthy, that they live in and eat dirt, seems unfair to many. If their sparse bristly hair and flat snout do not accord with human ideals of beauty, it is hardly reason enough to brand them unclean. Pigs, in fact display remarkable similarities to human beings, in their behaviour. Many farmers maintain that, of all the farm animals, pigs are most like humans in building rudimentary family units. Monogamous and sometimes lifelong bonds can emerge between adult pigs. Sows care for their piglets long after other animals have left young to fend for themselves, and hogs vigorously defend their 'wife and children' from other pigs. What is more, physiologically and anatomically speaking, the closest animal to humans is the pig. Fire-services use pig carcasses in place of human corpses in burning-building simulations because their physical make-up is so similar to our own. We even use pig hearts for transplantation into humans.

Most Muslim schools of thought adhere to the general interpretation that all creatures from the ocean are thought to be *halal*. Hanafi Sunnis, the majority of Muslims, follow essentially the same laws of Kashrut, the Jewish dietary laws. Both believe that only fish with scales and fins are acceptable. Shi'ites also follow this rule, but make an exception for some crustaceans, for example, shrimps and prawns.

CHAPTER 18

Christmas or Eid?

At no time in the Islamic year is food more important than during feast days, when it is the duty of every Muslim to share food and drink with others, to invite those on their own, to welcome those less fortunate. Charity is also essential. Long before the day of Eid, special donations are collected for the poor known as Zakat al-Fitr, made to ensure everyone can afford to take part in the festivities and have some money left over to buy a new pair of shoes. Many Muslims send money to friends or family members in other countries. On Islamic feast days it is customary to sacrifice an animal using the *halal* method of slaughter, whether sheep or goat.

Just as Christians have two major annual celebrations, Christmas and Easter, Muslims also have two central feasts, Eid al-Fitr, which takes place at the end of Ramadan, and Eid al-Adha, the feast of sacrifice that happens during the *hajj* pilgrimage to Mecca. Like Christmas and New Year, both Eid feasts provide the opportunity for friends and family to get together to celebrate and offer thanks to God. The word '*eid*' or '*id*' is Arabic and means 'returning often': it represents the idea of renewal, a time for new beginnings. Both feasts award a sense of unity to Muslims all over the world.

The most important festival in the Muslim calendar is the Eid al-Adha, meaning 'the main Eid'. It is held in memory of Abraham's willingness to sacrifice his son Ishmael at God's command. The festival of Eid al-Adha, above all, symbolises the idea of sacrifice and renewal of faith. For those pilgrims on *hajj* at Mecca, the sacrifice is physically represented with the sacrifice of an animal.

Eid al-Fitr or Eid Ramadan is slightly shorter than the four days holiday taken for Eid al-Adha, and so is sometimes referred to as the minor eid, or little festival, in Arabic, Eid al-Sagheer. In Muslim countries everyone has three days of holiday, and in the UK Muslims take one day for prayer, partying and eating. It takes place at the end of the month of Ramadan and is a great climax as well as release after a long month of fasting. As soon as the new moon is sighted at the end of the month, the fast is broken, often by eating just a date or apricot, or taking a fruit drink. Then there is a meal later on, to which guests are invited and for which food is cooked in huge amounts. In stricter Muslim families there is a prayer, and in Muslim countries such is the release of emotion that everyone congratulates each other with '*Eid Mubarak*'. Delicious sweets are handed round, decorations are put up, and cards given to friends and family.

At Eid there is no call to prayer. Muslims are supposed to take a bath or shower, and dress in their best clothes, and then go to a special Eid prayer an hour after sunrise at their local mosque. Mosques at this time are packed, and in Muslim countries there are so many people trying to get to prayer that some countries set up Eid *gahs*, or open-air mosques, in parks or fields, or even car parks. The Eid prayer usually consists of two *rak'as* and extra *takbirs* or sayings of *Allahu Akbar*. There is also usually a sermon, and other prayers before noon. Afterwards there is hugging and kissing, and gifts are given. At midday a great feast is usually served to friends and family and the feasting goes on late into the night.

In addition to the two major Eid festivals, various other events are commemorated by Muslims throughout the year. Muharram, the first month in the Islamic year, celebrates the departure of Muhammad to Medina, the *Hirja*, the date of which is recognised as the beginning of the spread of Islam. 1 Muharram, New Year's Day, has a special significance for Muslims, and, just as in non-Muslim tradition, resolutions are made. Originally the Day of Atonement in the Jewish calendar, Ashura falls on the tenth of Muharram, and is a day of mourning, as well as of fasting for many Muslims. It is a symbol of sacrifice. It is also perhaps best known for commemorating the day when Hussain, grandson of the Prophet Muhammad, was martyred at Kerbela in 61 AH. Shi'ites wear black as a sign of mourning for the first ten days before Ashura, and then on the tenth replay the bloody scenes of suffering and death of Hussain.

On the 10th of Muharram, Shi'ite men process behind a white horse and alongside floats known as *tazias*, and some even beat themselves with chains and cut themselves as a sign of honour. Ashura also commemorates a number of other events, such as the birth of Adam, the creation of the seven heavens, the birth of Abraham, and the day on which he almost sacrificed his son Ishmael, as well as the day Jesus was born. It is also said by Muslims that it will mark the Day of Judgement, although a Muslim should not concern themselves with when that day will be.

It is not just days that are sacred in the Muslim calendar. Certain nights are equally significant; and on these occasions in some Muslim countries mosques are lit up for the entire night. *Laylat al-Isra wal-Miraj*, on 27 Rajab, celebrates the Prophet Muhammad's Night Journey to Jerusalem and through the seven heavens.

Another important evening in the Islamic calendar is the *Laylat al-Bara'at*. It is said that on this night, known as the Night of Blessing, at the full moon before the beginning of Ramadan, God orders who will live and who will die, and who will be forgiven or condemned for the coming year. It celebrates Muhammad's preparations for Ramadan, during which he would pray for entire nights; and so many Muslims also spend the night in prayer. They do the same on the *Laylat al-Quadr*, the Night of Power, on the 27th of Ramadan, the night of Muhammad's first revelation, and the holiest of nights for all Muslims.

All feasts and festivals provide a focal point for fun, celebration and togetherness in all societies, but the co-existence of different customs in our mixed societies can also be a source of strife. While Muslims accept the Virgin birth, they do not accept the Trinity. To this avail, some Muslims living in the West have said that they feel uneasy about the emphasis placed on traditional Christian cele-brations. Some have even insisted that non–Christian greetings cards should be issued at these times, and that city Christmas lights should represent no Christian imagery. Recent efforts to placate such groups by introducing non-doctrinal carols have infuriated non-Muslims, who argue that traditional cultural customs that have been in place for centuries are being eroded. However, the majority of Muslims say they do not feel uncomfortable and that it is only for rigid individuals that carols at Christmas and nativity plays present a problem.

CHAPTER 19

Drink, drugs and rock 'n' roll

One of the obstacles to harmony between Muslim and non-Muslim at any festival time is the issue of alcohol. Just as meat that is considered unclean is forbidden to Muslims, so is any substance that is deemed to have an intoxicating effect. The religious basis of this somewhat austere outlook is that God is the owner of our bodies, and anything that is harmful to our physical or mental wellbeing is disrespectful to his creation, impedes our ability to worship him properly, and is therefore held as *haram*. Any substance that encourages the inhibitions to be cast off, results in a loss of control over the emotions, or presents an impediment to clear thought, is normally eschewed by Muslims. In some parts of the Muslim world, not only alcohol and drugs, but music, dancing, and even poetry are frowned upon, capable as they are of enlivening and intoxicating the spirit. It is said that the Prophet also disliked music for its propensity to inflame the passions, although music is not banned in the Qur'an. Instead, it is left to a person's conscience.

Wine was commonly consumed during the Prophet's lifetime, and had been a part of the culture since antiquity.

In Yemen, a type of mead was drunk, with or without food. Alcohol was also used in medicines, where it was an ingredient in many cures and palliative concoctions. Drunkenness was accepted as part of daily life, and date wine was to the Arabs what a glass of Merlot is to us today.

The instructions from God with regard to intoxicating substances are sometimes considered as slightly confusing, but variances are derived from the fact that they happened gradually in Muhammad's continuing revelations. As a result, the Qur'an's teachings regarding alcohol can be difficult to pin down. One of the problems has always been translation, not least concerning what even constitutes an alcoholic drink or an intoxicating substance. The word used in the Qur'an, *khamr*, meaning hidden or covered, can describe several different types of drink, not all of which are alcoholic. This has led to the adoption of varying standards in different Muslim societies.

In Muhammad's first revelation alcohol is regarded as nourishing, but at the same time harmful. 'From the fruits of the date palm and the vine you can derive wholesome fruit and drink. Behold there is a sign in this for the wise.' A later revelation indicated that the problems of *khamr* outweighed the good. 'When they ask you concerning wine and gambling, say: 'In them is great sin and little profit; but the sin is greater than the profit.' Next came the suggestion of the wickedness of intoxicating substances in terms of their interference with prayer. 'O believers! Do not come to prayer with a befogged mind, but come when you can fully understand all that you are saying (*surah* 4:43).' Finally, some time later, came the outright prohibition: 'O believers! Intoxicants, gambling, and trying to foretell the future are the lures of Satan; if you wish to prosper, you must keep away from these things. It is Satan's plan to stir up enmity and hatred in your midst with them (*surah* 5: 90).' If it had been assumed previously that there were advantages to drinking alcohol, it was from then on understood that these were outweighed by other considerations. Alcohol immediately became *haram*.

Most Muslims agree that the sayings of the Prophet underline his disapproval of the use of alcohol, even in medicine. According to more than one *hadith*, he referred to it as a disease, only to be taken if absolutely necessary One of the most quoted, by Tirmidhi, states that 'Allah has cursed *khamr*, those who produce it, those for whom it is produced, those who drink it, those who serve it, those who carry it, those it is carried to, those who sell it, and those who buy it.' The message here seems unequivocal: Muslims, whatever their school of thought, are not allowed to drink at any time 'in order to feel the click', as Tennessee Williams put it.

However, the fact remains that there exist many *hadith*s relating to drinking, expressing many different points of view which are all too often contradictory, and certain schools of Islam have used different interpretations of the sayings of Muhammad on the subject. It is the definition of what constitutes an alcoholic drink that provides most of the material for debate. When drinking is condemned, the precise drinks included in its prohibition tend to be determined by custom, rather than by any appeal by the Qur'an. These customs are normally derived from the precedents set by Muhammad and his companions, as described in the *hadith*s.

The commonest definition of *khamr* is substance that affects judgement, personality, and concentration – and hence the ability to pray. Any quantity of such a substance is forbidden. Some Muslims interpret this strictly: those who follow the teachings of the Shafi'is and Malikis would insist that no drop of alcohol should ever cross a Muslim's lips. Those who follow the Hanafi school, however, have a more accommodating attitude. Their arguments are based on subtleties of the Arabic language, and are often not concordant with the literature. They are often accused by others of employing legal and linguistic sophistry in order to legitimise some alcoholic drinks. Hanafis originally believed that grape juice allowed to ferment was *khamr*, but that other alcoholic beverages were allowed. This view has since been dropped in favour of an outright ban, though Hanafis do allow the use of alcohol in cough syrups and other oral medications.

As with the problems the Islamic jurists found in defining alcoholic drinks, so there are difficulties even in separating the terminology that describes smoking from that which applies to drinking. In Turkish, Pashto, and Arabic there are, for instance, standard terms covering the practices involved both in drinking and smoking: it is the context that determines meaning. In Iran, the same Farsi word may cover either drinking or eating.

After the time of the Prophet, Islamic law continued to be damning about alcohol, although there was no specific penalty for drinking laid down in the Qur'an. At a time when flogging was the mildest punishment for slander and other forms of abuse, it is surprising that it only applied to drinkers if they became disorderly or disruptive. Drinking without misbehaviour would then have merited a lesser punishment. Muhammad had said that if a person was flogged for possession of alcohol, it was because they were breaking the law of the land rather than Islamic law. By the eighth century, vineyards and wineries throughout the Muslim world were abandoned, such was the abhorrence of alcohol. Its use in medicine, common since the days of ancient Rome and Athens, was banned. It was also forbidden in the kitchen.

Nowadays, off-licences may be out of the question in the Middle East, but even though it is not openly for sale in most countries (there are exceptions – Egypt, for example) alcohol is fairly widely drunk, anyway. In many places, non-Muslim minorities sell it discreetly to those desirous of a drink, and at parties behind closed doors, even among Muslims, it is not unusual for alcohol to be freely offered. That said, alcohol traders often suffer severe recriminations during times of civil unrest: in the Islamic revolution in Iran, and during the riots in Baghdad, pictures of alcohol traders' premises being burnt, and of whisky bottles being smashed, appeared in the international press. In some countries today, where the rules about drinking alcohol are rigorously enforced, the penalties are not only as severe as, but are even heavier than, they once were. In Saudi Arabia, the penalties for expatriate workers distilling alcohol are as fierce as at any time in history.

Alcohol is not the only substance commonly accepted by non-Muslims that is strictly forbidden by Islam. As with alcohol, it is the anti-social effect of taking any type of recreational drug that is evil. Sheikh ibn Taymiyya, a Sunni Islamic scholar born in what is now Turkey, suggested that,

'Sinful people smoke hashish because they find it produces rapture and delight, an effect similar to drunkenness . . . it promotes dullness and lethargy, it disturbs the mind and temperament, excites sexual desire, and leads to shameless promiscuity.' The reality is that drugs have been in use in Islamic societies, as in non-Muslim ones, since antiquity, and in the early centuries of Islam illegal drugs such as opium, hashish, and *qat* were traded by merchants along the Silk Route. Today, despite more than 1,400 years of Islamic rule, the drug problem has not gone away. On the contrary, heroin has become the principal cash crop in Afghanistan, and the country is now one of the most prolific producers of heroin in the world. Although during the rule of the Taliban the crop was illegal, the harvest has flourished since they were overthrown. Afghan heroin has created appalling problems in other Middle Eastern countries, particularly in urban areas such as Tehran in Iran.

In Muslim quarters, hashish is condemned universally. However, at least until the 1960s, it was for centuries firmly associated with Middle Eastern Islamic countries. First derived from a word of Egyptian or Syrian origin (*khashkhash* in Arabic signifies simply 'poppy'), hashish was actually taken long before Muhammad's lifetime. In Constantinople, it was known by the name of *asrar*, which means a secret preparation. The cultivation of the plant was continued in many parts of the former Ottoman Empire, and thrived in Mesopotamia, especially near Mosul. Dealers in hashish would return to their plantations towards the end of May to examine their crop, inspect the plants, and make any improvements to their cultivation. Merchants sent their workers into the fields to cut off the heads of the plants so that the concentration of the drug in the leaves would be increased. Fifteen days after the heads were cut off, the plants were harvested. The leaves were stripped in sheds, then spread out to dry upon a long coarse carpet made of wool, called a *kitm*.

In the eighteenth century, the taking of *hashish* was still widespread in Islamic countries. British travellers at that time describe the use of *sheera* or *bing* – the leaves of hemp, the cannabis plant – in the region when, just as today, the leaves were processed into small lozenges, mixed with tobacco, and smoked. It was said that the people ruined by succumbing to the temptation to smoke hashish were no better than beasts tempted by demons. In Syria and Egypt it was not so often smoked, but was taken in a fatty form rather like butter. In Turkey, it was sold in the form of a syrup, in pastilles, smoked in water pipes, or mixed with tobacco. Cigars could be impregnated with it. It was also frequently smoked through a hookah, and, just as in student parties today, it could also be mixed with food, chewed, or drunk in an infusion like tea. Other users blended hashish with opium or coffee and made a mousse known as *barsh*. Today *hashish* is just as common in the Levant, but is still always carefully concealed, with smokers pretending that their cigarettes contain only tobacco.

Cannabis was another forbidden substance in Islam. It had been introduced as a recreational drug from India and Persia in the twelfth century, but its history in the Middle East predates this time – and even predates Islam – though its use was then medicinal. It had been given to some women to ease the pain of childbirth as far back as the second millennium BC. In recent times, the grave of a

Palestinian woman who died in childbirth was found to contain traces of cannabis.

Drugs, like alcohol, are a problem in any society, but are avoided by most Muslims today. Prohibitions against coffee-drinking and smoking, however, are not nearly so rigorously obeyed, and only the strictest Muslims regard such infusions as *khamr*. Coffee and, to a lesser extent, tea, are in many people's minds synonymous with the Middle East, and few people who have visited the area do not recall being served with memorably strong, sweet coffee. Not many people realise, however, that according to some Muslims their hosts may have been breaking strict Islamic law in offering the beverage.

Coffee has a very long and interesting relationship with Islam. For those non-Muslims who regard their daily cappuchino before work as being harmless as a glass of water, this can seem baffling. It seems difficult to believe it was once said of coffee that – in any quantity – it rendered a man 'incapable of distinguishing a man from a woman or the earth from the heavens'. Even so, coffee is by far the commonest addiction in the West today, albeit, we believe, a relatively innocuous one. In centuries gone by, however, the definition of what actually constituted an intoxicating substance in Islam made coffee a topic of heated debate. Many Muslims regarded the drink as intoxicating, and therefore unlawful, while others disputed this, saying that it had the virtue of keeping those who drank it awake, and was therefore a valuable aid to the pious in their nocturnal devotions. Nowadays opposition to the harmful effects of coffee has faded in many quarters of Muslim society, and attempts to ban it have generally met with little success.

As time passed and coffee continued to be drunk, without suspicion of its being seriously intoxicating, only the strictest Muslims forbade its use. While it was clear that coffee had an effect on the mental state, this did not seem to be a detrimental one. Muslims who advocated coffee never denied this, but quoted the effect as being a good reason to drink it. Al-Jaziri, for example, one of the great Arab commentators on coffee, gave a summary of its benefits, describing the effect of large quantities: 'It brings to the drinker a sprightliness of spirit and a sense of mental well-being.' In and around the Arabian peninsula, where coffee drinking began, there is even a word, *marqaha*, describing the slight euphoria caffeine induces.

In the past, coffee houses did not only come under fire for serving coffee. The larger ones provided physical comforts of every kind, including small indoor gardens replete with cooling fountains surrounded by luxurious cushions and pillows. They were a haven from the dirt, smell, and noise of the streets outside, their cool ambience ensuring a regular trade. However, while the coffee houses of Europe and America became centres of political intrigue, and refuges for the powerful, those in Middle Eastern Islamic societies became known as forums of bawdy talk and moral turpitude, where gangs of wastrels would lounge around fountains all day, playing board games and neglecting their prayers. Some of them even housed gambling dens – a vice strictly forbidden by Islam. Live entertainment was a popular strategy for attracting customers: puppeteers, musicians and story-tellers became commonplace. Treatises slammed the practice of entertainment, stating that it contributed to a general atmosphere of indulgence and debauchery. In the minds of the pious, these establishments became repugnant – perhaps rightly so, for they eventually attracted the prostitutes and gamblers that had populated pre-Islamic taverns in Mesopotamia, coming all the time closer and closer to resembling those earlier dens of iniquity, in aspect and clientele. Services that were an affront to the social and religious standards of the day became freely available.

Sufis have been accused of abusing far worse substances than coffee. Although most claim that the *zikr*, their remembrance of God, should be attributed to divine inspiration, it is widely believed that some mind-altering substances were resorted to – and still are – for the purpose of exciting the intellect, to encourage it to produce visions, or, we would say, hallucinations. A Sufi's intention when using hashish is evidently not to use it as a stimulant, but rather as a spiritual soporific capable of producing a quiescence of the soul known as *kaif.* It has always been known that mixing other narcotics with hashish produces a delirium worse than that engendered by opium alone. Regular users of these mixtures developed tolerance to them: the dose had to be progressively increased, both to satisfy a craving, and to achieve the sense of beatitude.

Although many of the great mystical Sufi poets used the metaphor of intoxication, this was never intended to be an endorsement of substances banned by Islam. While some Sufis are known for their belief that drinking wine expands their minds and enables them to make better contact with God, other Muslims – and most other Sufis – see this as nothing more than an excuse to get drunk. Those following Sufi teaching – then, as now – abhor the use of intoxicants or hallucinogens. Their effects are illusory, say most Sufis; the only way to truly know God is through earnest prayer.

For the vast majority of Muslims today, it remains the case that alcohol and other drugs are totally out of bounds, while in general tea, coffee, and tobacco are tolerated or freely enjoyed. Ultimately, the pre-eminent consideration when deciding if a substance is *haram* or not is the extent to which it frees the user from inhibitions and undermines self-control. If it interferes with rational thought, or, worse, prayer, then it is likely to be considered unacceptable to Muslims, who regard knowing one's limits, and behaving appropriately, to be of paramount importance in the service of God.

CHAPTER 20

The creatures of God

If Muslims can feel uncomfortable with their non-Muslim neighbours who drink heavily at seasonal celebrations, further tensions have arisen regarding the rites and rituals surrounding Islamic feast days. Such people argue that the *halal* method of slaughter used at Muslim festivals such as Eid is cruel and barbaric. They say that cutting the jugular vein with a sharp knife is not always kind to the animal specifically because the process is not always carried out with the level of skill required. Assuming the slaughter is done properly, Muslims insist that cutting the throat with a sharp knife is the only humane, as well as the most hygienic, method of slaughter. It is not the fault of Islam if individuals do not abide by the rules as ordained by God Himself. Like errant sheep, they have strayed from the spirit of what Islam really intended.

There can be no doubt that according to the Islamic sources the Prophet Muhammad was kind to all animals, and that his concern extended to those that had been reared for the table. Those animals should be slaughtered, he said, so that they suffered the least pain possible, and all stages of the process should be conducted with maximum humanity. If a beast is inhumanely slaughtered, the meat should be considered no better than carrion and, according the law, not fit for human consumption. Ancient Muslims were taught that before a beast was killed, it must be out of the sight of other animals and their young. They should be isolated from the herd, just as a park ranger isolates the deer that is to be shot to provide venison for the estate.

Islam also set standards for governing the care of animals awaiting slaughter. Animals should have comfortable resting places and plenty of water to drink. They should have their needs provided for at all stages of life. While young and active, the male should have access to the female during the natural mating season. Nor, unlike common practice in non-Muslim societies, was consideration for their welfare suspended just because the animals had passed their prime. Rather, they should continue to be cared for humanely, even if they were no longer fit to carry loads or to be ridden.

It remains the case, however, that the image of stray mongrels roaming around the streets in Islamic countries, unwatered, unfed, and unloved, is one that has defined how we see the Islamic attitude towards animals. It is not entirely fair, since the abuse children dole out to these wretched beasts is decidedly un-Islamic – yet it persists, and is widespread. Images in the media have reinforced this stereotype. But in the case of the noble beasts of burden, particularly those who play some important role, great care is taken to meet their needs. After a ride, a horse must be groomed, fed, and watered before the rider tends to himself. That said, the approach is now quite unsentimental, and once the horse is no longer able to carry out its duties, it will commonly be sold or put down.

The treatment of domestic animals in non-Muslim society varies widely. Many children are taught that animals are as much God's creation as people. They may or may not have a soul, but they are at all times to be treated with compassion and kindness. Whilst this is also true in the Islamic world, Muslims do not regard animals as surrogate human beings. The pampered pooch in Chelsea, with the immaculately trimmed coat, manicured claws and fancy food – a lifestyle and condition better than the majority of children in the developing world – would be regarded as an aberration. Creatures fit to grace the tables at Crufts can be found the Muslim societies, particularly in Beirut or Egypt, whether they are a pampered pet or a valued working animal, but the treatment afforded them has more to do with the financial position of the owner than any religious consideration.

There are many prescriptions made in Islam for the respect, welfare, and treatment of animals. Muslims not only have a duty of guardianship over the planet, they are responsible for the well-being of all the creatures that inhabit it since, although animals are God's creation, they are incapable of free will. The Qur'an teaches that animals, like us, are part of God's great family. It says, 'Do you not see that it is God whose praises are celebrated by all beings in the heavens and on earth, even by the birds in their flocks? (*surah* 24: 41).' God regards man and animals differently, but both are of value to Him. In the Qur'an, Allah holds that the dog trotting along beside his owner is valued alongside its master. Perhaps more surprising is that God gives the snake or caterpillar the same status as the dog or horse. The Qur'an states: 'Allah has created every animal from water: of them there are some that creep on their bellies, some that walk on two legs, and some that walk on four (*surah* 24:25).'

Muhammad's behaviour toward animals set the model example to Muslims. We know from the *hadith*s and the *sunnah* that Muhammad was always extremely kind to them, not only treasuring his cat, but caring for the birds and even the insects on which they fed. A saying attributed to the Prophet sums up his opinion: 'Whoever is kind to the creatures of God, is kind to himself.' A quote from another *hadith*, according to Kashf al-Khafa, reports that the Prophet once said, 'All creatures are God's dependants, and the most beloved to God among them is he who does good to God's dependants.'

Although there are, strictly speaking, no favourites, Muhammad was reputed to have been a great lover of cats, which is one reason they are found all over the Middle East today. One day, when Muhammad was preaching to his companions, he was cradling a cat in his arms while he spoke to them. On another occasion, the Prophet was resting when a cat came and sat down beside him. It went to sleep on Muhammad's cloak, and the Prophet, when he needed to move, was reluctant to disturb it, as it looked so peaceful. Rather than wake it, the Prophet cut away part of his own cloak. It is said that when Muhammad returned home at the end of that day, the warmth of the cat's welcome so delighted him that he decreed, somewhat capriciously perhaps, that from then onwards cats should be treated with special regard. It is said that the cat awoke and bowed his head in gratitude, upon which the Prophet stroked him three times, thus assuring him of a permanent place in Paradise. It is even said that a cat saved Muhammad's life, having moved a deadly snake, concealed in the Prophet's coat, so as to reveal it.

No aspect of God's entire creation is overlooked in the holistic Islamic world-view. God also respects animals that are often considered repellent by humans. Muhammad told of an ancient, earlier prophet who was stung by an ant and as an act of revenge commanded that the ants and their nest should be destroyed. God was offended by this cruelty and reprimanded him by saying, 'Because one ant stung you, you burned a whole community that glorified Me.'

Although Muhammad regarded cats as pure animals, non-Muslims are often dismayed by his teaching that dogs are unclean. Even so, he taught that dogs should also be well cared for. Birds are as important as mammals. The Qu'ran tells how some companions of the Prophet seized chicks from the nest of a bird that had been unwisely built too close to ground. When Muhammad saw that the mother bird had been driven by her grief to hover above them, he asked who had so distressed the bird by taking her young. Muhammad ordered them to return the fledglings to the nest.

This love of animals according to Islam has been reflected in the arts and literature of its cultures for centuries. Animals are depicted as sources of wisdom from which humans can learn. In classic Arabic literature, there are over 600 words for lion, camel, and horse, illustrating the great importance that Islamic society accorded them.

Bestiaries were compiled, as in the West —one by Jahiz, writing in the fourteenth century, was of seven volumes in which animals, described as wonders of God's creation, are shown to symbolise facets of human nature. It was not only the written word that extolled the importance of the animal kingdom. The visual arts featured lions, gazelles, cats, birds, and fish. Carvings of animals have decorated important Islamic buildings, despite their not strictly being acceptable forms of decoration.

Today Islamic law accords animals rights, unlike the teaching of both the Old and New Testaments which have little positive to say about animals. Typical of the Islamic laws protecting the welfare of animals is the Prophet's instruction to his followers that they should not inflict any unnecessary pain on them; nor should they take pleasure in activities that might result in their injury. Muhammad also gave specific guidelines on hunting, and on the pursuit of wild animals. Among the cruelties he prohibited was the use of animals in sport, particularly as targets of blood sports. It is unlikely that the sons of the British Raj in India ever knew that the way they hunted tigers would not only now outrage modern society, but would have been outlawed by the Prophet 1,400 years ago.

Animals are to be protected not only from the cruelty of man, but from the behaviour of other animals, whether of their own species or of another. It is the duty of a shepherd to make certain that his flock is protected, to avoid the misery of being gored or bitten being inflicted by one animal on another. In this respect Islam seems way ahead of civil laws in non-Muslim states. It is only in the past fifty years or so in Europe that animals have been dehorned in order to save the rest of the herd from damaging wounds. Any activity that encourages an animal to fight with another, such as cock or dog fighting, is forbidden in Islam. Although the quarry differs from one culture to another, the principle remains the same. One *hadith* (al-Nisai, Ibn Hibban) reads, 'If someone kills a sparrow for sport, the sparrow will cry out on the Day of Judgement: 'O Lord! That person killed me for nothing!' One may take the life of an animal only if it is for a genuinely useful purpose, such as to eat.

Hunting has been as much part of the culture of the desert as it has of the British countryside, since long before the time of the Prophet. In the lands of Arabia, from the onset of Islam, hunting has been allowed, but the way the hunt was conducted has always been carefully controlled. Special mention is made under Islamic law of not allowing animals to be killed by having their bones broken, such as is still the practice in parts of Southern Europe. Animals used for hunting should be well trained. In order to ensure a clean kill, the animal should be speared, shot, or killed by another animal been bred and trained for this task. If the hunter is able to approach the animal while it is still alive it should be slaughtered just as one would slaughter a domestic animal. It has always been forbidden to hunt if the intention is not to kill the animal, but to capture it. This would have outlawed many English eighteenth- and nineteenth-century hunts which pursued a carted stag. (At the end of the hunt, the stag was captured and taken back to its paddock to be hunted on another day.) If a weapon is used, it must be efficient and sharp to ensure a clean and speedy kill.

Clubbing or hitting an animal is unacceptable in most cultures. Nothing can excuse acts of violence towards an innocent animal, or hunting to extinction simply to satisfy the vanity of humans. Similarly cruel methods of factory-farming are forbidden. No animal should be kept in crowded conditions or force-fed. Anything that forces an animal to grow unnaturally, or to have its life artificially shortened, is forbidden; likewise, experiments aimed at developing luxury face-creams, for instance. Using animals in scientific experiments that make a positive contribution to human medical research are allowed only if the animals are well looked after and their suffering is minimised.

Carnivores are considered to be in a different category from herbivores. Eating or killing such animals is generally forbidden, or at least disapproved of. An exception might be made to such prohibitions if the carnivore was a threat to humans, livestock, crops, or property, but their meat is not eaten. This dictate excludes pests and predators. It has always been acceptable in Muslim countries to kill animals such as wolves, rats, or scorpions, and provision is made for this even while on pilgrimage.

CHAPTER 21

Friends of the earth

It is not just animals that are God-given, and that man has a responsibility to look after properly. According to Islam, the existence of everything in nature, whether animate or inanimate, praises God and is in harmony with Him. The Qur'an states that, 'There is not a thing but celebrates His praise, and yet you understand not how they declare His glory.' Muslims believe that God created the world, and, as it is an expression of His omnipotence, it is not for man to interfere with His will. God determines when and if the rain should fall and the sun shine. The effects of the elements upon the world are also His will, and it is for mankind to make the best use they can of what they are given. God created the desert, just as He created the green oases of plants and water in fertile land. Everything is held in perfect balance, and the aim for any Muslim is that this balance and harmony of nature should be preserved, in accordance with the will of God.

God, in granting man reason and the ability to behave rationally, to learn the lessons from past generations, and to pass them on, expects him to maintain the planet. God has made man His *khalifah*, which, if translated, literally means His stewards, or agents, who must care for the planet. In the Qur'an, this special charge is referred to as *al amanah*, 'the trust'. It is written that this great responsibility was refused by the mountains, and by the rest of creation, but taken on by humans, in their folly. Muslims – and many non-Muslims – argue that the prevalent competitive, greedy, materialistic culture ignores the responsibility that God has bestowed on mankind: an avaricious and decadent lifestyle is undermining the environment. This has upset the harmony between man and nature, and therefore between man and God.

As in Genesis, the Qur'an states, 'It is He who created the heavens and the earth, according to a plan and with a purpose.' God 'raised up the heavenly canopy without any visible support. Then He established Himself on the throne of authority and made the sun and the moon subservient to His laws.' Even those who do not believe in divine creation must admit that the natural world is astonishing in its complexity and ingenuity. The Qur'an uses the simile that creation is like a set of scales originally crafted in Heaven: if the harmony of nature is not to be disturbed, this carefully balanced system must not be interfered with in any way. The Qu'ran repeatedly stresses the need to maintain the equilibrium that was initially determined by God Himself. One *surah* puts it thus: 'The sun and the moon rotate in ordered orbits, the plants and the trees, too, do obeisance. The firmament – He raised it high, and set the balance of everything, so that you [humanity] may not upset the balance. Keep the balance with equity and fall not short in it.'

As a result, Muslims have an ethical approach to the environment that would satisfy the greenest of ecological activists. They are duty bound to be as self-sufficient as possible, not to be wasteful, and not to abuse the earth so as to damage it for future generations. It is said that, come the Day of Judgement, God will expect people to account for the way in which they have respected His creation, and show what they did to treat it well while it remained in their trust. The Qur'an says, 'Do no mischief on the earth after it hath been set in order, but call on Him with fear and longing, for the Mercy of Allah is always near to those who do good.'

Shari'ah law, perhaps surprisingly, includes legislation about ecology that, although drawn up more than fourteen centuries ago, has just as much relevance today. The original law is based on a number of verses in the Qur'an and the sayings of the Prophet, such as, 'The world is green and beautiful, and God has appointed you as his stewards over it. He sees how you acquit yourselves.' One *hadith* recorded by Abu Muslim, states, 'Whoever plants a tree and looks after it with care, until it matures and becomes productive, will be rewarded in the Hereafter' – an aim that, if pursued by modern town-planners, would greatly improve the appearance of many urban areas. Other quotes from the *hadith*s of Bukhari and Muslim reinforce this message: 'If anyone plants a tree or sows a field and men, beasts, or birds eat from it, he should consider it as a charity on his part.'

It was similarly recorded that the Prophet Muhammad prohibited the cutting of any tree in the desert that provided shade or sustenance for humans or animals.

Another tradition tells that when Muhammad lived in Medina, he ordered that the trees in and around the city should be protected (*Mishkat al-Masabih*). He decreed that they should not be cut down, and that their leaves should not be stripped off them unless they were needed for fodder. In the early medieval period, Muslim scholars introduced similar laws for the conservation of forests, as well as individual trees, and protected them from being felled for grazing – a lesson that would be applicable today in many parts of South America.

The heartlands of Islam – the Arabian peninsula, Syria, Persia, Mesopotamia, north and north-west Africa, and southern Spain – have always been areas of intense sun and sparse rainfall, with extremes of heat and drought. Egypt, Mesopotamia, and India have all benefited from their major rivers, but other areas, lacking great rivers, built on pre-Islamic techniques to achieve ingenious methods of water distribution through skilful engineering and mathematical calculation. Early Muslim scientists required wit and patience to build their networks. Great dams were constructed, such as that outside Marrakesh in Morocco, and that near Qayrawan in Tunis. Water-cooling systems were devised from the earliest times, making use of wind and the cooling effects of evaporation. Over the centuries, wind towers became a great feature of urban architecture in the desert areas of Persia.

Water, whether from a natural spring, a well, or from rain, is one of the main symbols of purity and life in Islam. It should not be wasted, even when it is used to prepare for prayer on the bank of an abundantly flowing river. Water is considered symbolic of life itself. It fulfills the same cooling, refreshing, and purifying role in the garden as it does in the ablutions. The Qur'an often emphasises the importance of water and its life-giving properties. It explains how water fashions every living thing, and is promised in abundance to the faithful in Paradise. The 'shades and fountains, and such fruits as their hearts desire', mentioned repeatedly in the Qur'an as a feature of Paradise, frequently figure in the design of Islamic royal gardens throughout the Muslim world. There are also detailed practical lessons concerning the correct use and distribution of water. Both freshwater and seawater are frequently mentioned, and the contrast between fresh, sweet and pleasant drinking water and the salty sea water is emphasised. The richness of the language in the Qur'an used to describe water is significant: vivid adjectives such as 'purifying', 'blissful' and 'fresh', conveying the beauty of its animation and sound, abound.

Caring for water is not only wise and civilised, it is a form of worship. It is laid down by the Qur'an that water, a vital need, should be available to everyone. In addition, the sayings of the Prophet provide the basis upon which the particular Islamic laws about water were formulated. One, from al-Muwatta, advocates the virtue of sharing water with a dog. The basic principle is that water should never be squandered, wasted or polluted (hence it is forbidden to urinate in fresh or salt water). Any pollution that has a detrimental effect on animal, plant, or sea life disturbs the balance of God's world. If the water flows through undeveloped farmland, the stream is subject to different laws and customs. People are allowed access to it, to take off a certain amount to water their crops, and even to store some for a dry period. The longer the farm has been established, the greater their claim on its supply will be allowed. This ensures that the number of farms in any area is limited by the availability of water. Development is restricted or forbidden in areas around wells and streams: water is too precious a resource to leave unguarded. There are also areas of land that are declared to be reserves that need to be protected for the public good. These conservation areas are designated so as to encourage wildlife and trees, or to provide additional grazing space. Trespassers on land in a reserve are liable to be fined or jailed.

The Qur'an repeatedly attests that everything was created in order to worship God, and every creation praises Him. From flowers to insects to trees – everything resonates in constant harmony with the glory of God. Ruzbihan Baqli of Shiraz, a twelfth-century Muslim mystic, wrote that people can seek and find many answers to life's puzzles while contemplating three things – water, greenery, and a lovely face. Baqli was echoing the earlier thoughts of Rabi'a al-Adawiyya, known as Rabi'a of Basra, who, in mid-eighth century, while meditating one day, was called by her maidservant to look at the beauty of nature in spring, and to admire God's work in the garden. Rabi'a's reply – that the real gardens and flowers are within the heart, not without – was an interpretation of the garden that was to become prominent among later Muslim mystics.

Some of the most eloquent renderings of nature in poetry occur in the poetic verses of Jalal ud-Din Rumi, for whom gardens became the symbol of divine beauty. For Rumi, Allah is the Gardener, tending to his creation. The essential requirement for a good harvest is that the garden should be tended carefully, so that its beds are kept free of weeds and stones, and the soil is cultivated. The seeker of truth traverses this world by a stony path, and the burdens of life can break even the strongest nature. But, as water nourishes the rose, so does the beaten traveller, by submitting to the will of God, overcome his troubles.

In an earthly Islamic garden, every plant has a part to play in the recollection of God and even in prayer. They are symbolic of the beauty of God's creation, although an Islamic garden, whilst commanding a similar degree of awe, is a very different affair from an English cottage garden, with its narrow paths and beds thick at various times of the year with pansies, sweet williams, hollyhocks, daffodils, and snowdrops, and its disordered charm. It springs up of its own accord, year on year, and the best examples of this tumbledown aesthetic are looked upon with reverence and affection.

In a properly cultivated Islamic garden everything is held in balance by the geometry of the wall and the courtyard within. The wall has various roles, both symbolic and literal. These include defining the extent of the garden and providing privacy. Muslims have always valued personal privacy, and, with it, the privacy of women: they tend to be uncomfortable exposing their private life to strangers.

Behind the wall, Islamic gardens always follow a traditional pattern. In the richer parts of the Middle East, formal gardens, even on the steepest hillsides, are constructed with geometrical precision, their straight, measured lines reflecting the order of the Islamic universe. In larger formal gardens, long avenues of trees outline the straight paths, often leading to a summerhouse or pavilion at the end of the walkway. Narrow canals often widen out into tranquil pools with square, octagonal, cruciform, or shamrock-shaped ends. Larger and more formal Islamic gardens are known as *chahar-bagh*, a word derived from Old Persian and meaning 'four gardens'. *Chahar-bagh* recall the ancient division of the earth into four quarters. At the intersection of these divisions, a pavilion – or even a palace – often appears. In other *chahar-bagh*, the centrepiece might be a tree or pool. The four quarters are also often seen as reflections of the four rivers that flow through Paradise, thought to have inspired the architects who built the canals and pathways of Iran and Mughal India.

The more elaborate Islamic gardens contain intricate and interrelated shapes and colours. In the context of man-made precision, God's creation provides a counter-balance. Trees provide ever-changing patterns of shade. Flowers offer drifts of colour and scents. Wildlife adds to this causal harmony. Greenery in hot Islamic countries is all the more precious because of the difficulty of the terrain and climate. Spring in the desert is as magical as spring in more temperate climes. Within the confines of a garden, rose bushes, sweet-scented jasmine, almond, peach and apricot blossom give sanctuary to the lizards – and even the occasional goat.

The motif of worshipping God through nature is also reflected in the literature of many Islamic cultures. As far back as thirteenth-century Persia, 'Attar, the Turkish poet, praised the flowers of the garden, their colour, scent and shapes, citing native wild flowers, pointed tulips, and even tiny irises. Down the centuries the great poets of Islam have drawn on the imagery and symbolic power of trees, fruit and flowers to reflect the complexities of human spirit in relation to the Divine. As far back as the eighteenth century, the Afghan poet Rahman Baba extolled this quality in one of his great hymns: 'Every tree, and every shrub stand ready to bend before Him; Every herb and blade of grass is a tongue to utter His praise.' The trees were engaged in ritual prayer. and the birds in singing the litany, the violet bent down in prostration. On the same theme, Rumi wrote, 'See the upright position from the Syrian rose, and from the violet the genuflection, the leaf has attained prostration: refresh the call to prayer.'

Finally, and perhaps above all, the rose has been prized for centuries in Islamic gardens, primarily because it features heavily in Islamic religious symbolism. Its association with God, Moses, and the Prophet Muhammad gives it a special position in the Islamic garden, and in poetry. Poets consider the beauty and fragrance of the rose as a supreme example of the glory of Divine Creation. Sufis see it as representative of man's ultimate union with God – as in the well-known saying, 'He is in me, and I am in Him, like scent in the rosewater.'

Whether above or below, in actuality or in poetry, God's universe is praised for its beauty. Beauty, as seen in nature, is His gift from heaven and is created by God to please us. Ultimately, since God is beautiful, to love any beauty is to love God. This, Muslims say, is one of the basic tenets of the message of Islam.

CHAPTER 22

God's straight road

This heady notion of God's beauty in the world seems a distant cry from some of the hard issues facing the acceptance of Islam today in non-Muslim countries. In the twenty-first century, Shari'ah law in particular remains one of the great obstacles to the acceptance of Muslims into non-Muslim societies. One reason why a large Muslim population is not always welcomed is the suspicion that it will demand the installation of Shari'ah law, and that this will interfere with the long-established customs of the existing society. No sooner does the latest decision of a Shari'ah court, wherever it might be held in the world, appear in the Western press or in a television programme, than another fresh wave of anti-Islamic feeling sweeps the country. People brought up on British common law or the Napoleonic code of much of Europe are shocked by what many call Shari'ah law's barbaric criminal sentences, abhorrent to modern Western sensibilities. The difficulty that faces a multi-cultural society is to reconcile with the demands and expectations of twenty-first century life a system for judging human behaviour that was codified many centuries ago in the Middle East. Muslims themselves often disagree over the interpretation of the laws, so how can it ever find a place in our society?

Muslims who support Shari'ah argue that, if the country is not Islamic, the common law of the land in most Western secular societies is subject to human error; its purpose is to produce harmony in the population rather than to satisfy a religious code of conduct. It could be argued that the corpus of British legislature is based on Christian ideals, although it never claims to be divine law, nor even to be divinely inspired. Witnesses still swear on the Bible, judges attend religious services, bishops sit in Parliament, and there are prayers every day in the House of Commons. To Muslims, religion is the foundation of the civil process.

So what is Shari'ah exactly, and how does it function? The term Shari'ah itself means 'the road' or 'the straight way' in Arabic: what in English we would describe as 'the direct path' to God. Shari'iah law follows principles laid down by the Qur'an and the Prophet Muhammad 1,400 years ago. It is the divine law that determines the conduct for Muslim individuals and societies according to God's will, and as such, they believe, it is flawless. Many Muslims regard Shari'ah as the only way in which a society should be governed. They argue that the rioting seen recently in British cities highlights the fact that modern secular society has lost its way. Too many young people in Britain today, they say, have no real sense of belonging to or contributing positively to a community; and such criminality as has been seen recently would never occur if we were ruled by Shari'ah.

Shari'ah law presides over how Muslims should behave in every aspect of their domestic and professional lives, superseding any local laws. The definition of what law means in this context is very broad: while we might apprehend a judicial system as a network of prohibitions, Shari'ah also gives positive recommendations and instructions. It lays down how good Muslims should eat, sleep, and conduct their business affairs. If called upon, it dictates how they should serve in government, whether at a local or national level. Shari'ah law not only forbids universally recognised criminal acts such as theft or murder, but also prohibits such commercial practices as usury. It regulates the code of practice with regard to fasting, prayer, and charity. It is not just regarded by Muslims as something that orders the life of private individuals: it also pronounces on how public affairs are conducted. When administering criminal justice, it stipulates that the process must be transparent: nothing should be decided in secret, but the actions and decisions of the court must be public.

Although non-Muslims might find Islamic law difficult to understand and their court proceedings baffling, to those who are brought up with it the law seems to be transparent, and free of the bureaucracy endemic in many Western countries. In practice, however, this aspect of Shari'ah law is often ignored in the Muslim diaspora. Where local laws conflict with Shari'ah, there have been accusations of unofficial Shari'ah courts operating in local mosques with proceedings kept hidden from the authorities. Obviously this situation is untenable: no country can function with two disparate codes of justice struggling to prevail within its borders.

Muslims are not only bound by the Qur'an, but also by the *sunnah* and the *hadith*s. Although not part of the Qur'an itself, these represent the teachings of the Prophet Muhammad and must therefore be followed. Muslims resent the idea that they should replace their divine code by one that is determined by mere mortals. They point out that British law is not the law of an infallible God, but a system of law that is created by MPs sitting in Parliament, or by potentially fallible judges. Having said that, the *hadith*s were, of course, written by men, too. And it is from the *hadith*s and the *sunnah* that the majority of the details of Shari'ah are derived.

Most of the laws that now constitute the complex system of Shari'ah law became established by the third century after the Prophet's death, at about the time of the Norman Conquest in Britain. Although the principles of Shari'ah are laid down in the Qur'an, the detail is derived from the *sunnah*. The thousands of *hadith*s relevant to law were worked into legal texts in the early medieval period. The position after Muhammad's death was that any Muslim jurist or theologian could study an issue, apply reasoned thought to it (known as *ijtihad*), and then issue a non-binding opinion or verdict. In the early days of Islam there were hundreds of scholars, both men and women, all with followers and schools of thought. By the eleventh century, four major schools of thought (or *madhabs*) had emerged in Sunni Islam – the Hanifi, the Maliki, the Hanbali and the Shafi' – each named after the scholars that founded them. Thousands of students in each of the schools studied the law, interpreting it variously, developing along the way their own legal terminology.

In Shi'i Islam, two major schools of thought emerged – those of the Ja'fari and the Zaydi, as well as two minor ones, the Ibadi and the Thahiri. The result of this was that on each point of law there could be multiple opinions (*ikhtilaf*) and disagreement. Further disputes arose also regarding the necessary qualifications of those permitted to interpret the law. Sunnis then, as now, relied solely on the interpretations of the learned early jurists, whereas Shi'ites assert that living religious scholars are also entitled to act as interpreters, and in particular any living descendants of Fatima, the Prophet's daughter. So respected were (and are) such Islamic scholars, and so trusted were they where the law of Islam was concerned, that they were given the title of *ayatollah*, or 'sign of God'.

With such complexity regarding the evolution and interpretation of Shari'ah law, and with so many resulting differences of opinion, it is hardly surprising that many people find it hard to see the wood for the trees. Strict, orthodox Muslims argue that is precisely its complexity that renders Shari'ah a much more thorough, fair, and viable system. They continue to stress that Shar'iah is God's own law. As such, it holds everyone equal before it, and no one stands above it. They say that there is much more subtlety and detail in it than any other manmade systems of common law, and that it is never a question just of right and wrong. Five shades of what is morally acceptable and unacceptable separate what is allowed from what is forbidden, making for much greater nuance. *Fard* or *wajib* are acts that are compulsory according to the Qur'an, for example pilgrimage or fasting. *Mandub* or *Mustahab* are recommended acts, such as saying extra prayers during

Ramadan. *Mubah* are acts of conscience and principle. *Makruh* are those that are frowned on, but not actually out of bounds. Finally, *haram* constitutes anything prohibited under Islam, such as homosexuality or adultery.

Advocates of Shari'ah insist that, when properly administered, Islamic law is fair and merciful, despite its somewhat harsh appearance. They argue that Shari'ah is a fundamental part of each Muslim's life, and is not up for debate. There are compulsory human rights for anyone standing accused. They must have an unbiased court, and should not be presumed guilty unless this is proven. No one should be arrested and convicted or sentenced on the same day. All court proceedings must be held in public, and no one individual can be held accountable for the wrongdoings of others.

Those in favour of Shar'iah say that a Shari'ah court has a judge who is above reproach, as in any county or high court in England. However, in Shari'ah courts the judge's role is not to interpret the existing body of case law, and, if necessary, to amend or extend it, but rather to be a conduit for God's justice. As such, judges play the role of theologians and academic scholars, rather than legal experts. There can be no question of disputing a judicial opinion, nor of doubting the integrity of the judge. Islamic Law holds, as any good judge does, that any decision must be based on logical reasoning, but it can be influenced by other important factors, such as the person's previous record, character references from respected citizens, and a concern for the public good. The interpretation of mercy does not suppose that God expects courts invariably to acquit the prisoner. It means that God, who has a perfect sense of right and wrong and knows all the facts, will be ever merciful when it comes to the Day of Judgement. Even those who have committed the worst of sins will be treated kindly.

Many moderate Muslims, however, argue that the brand of Shari'ah law we observe today in many Muslim countries is very different from the basic moral compass set out in the Qur'an. Although the law itself is from God, Shari'ah, they argue, is the product of man's attempt to understand God's will over time. Its interpretation is human, and therefore inevitably full of failings.

CHAPTER 23

Crime and punishment

At first sight it seems to many non-Muslims hypocritical that the followers of a religion that has as one of its basic tenets the mercy of God demand the most draconian punishments for domestic, as well as criminal, misdemeanours in their everyday life in this world. The constant assertion that Islam is a merciful religion and is simply misunderstood by non-believers seems to be contradicted by images of criminals hanging from cranes, adulterous women being stoned to death, and thieves having their limbs amputated. Not only do the sentences strike horror into the hearts and minds of those brought up and, as they understand it, protected by a rigorously fair, if protracted, legal system, but the Islamic court proceedings seem to take place alarmingly fast, and without the safeguards and appeal systems of Western judicial system.

It is not just non-Muslims who attack the brutality of the Shari'ah penal system. Some moderate Muslims express just as much disgust at what are seen as medieval penalties of capital and corporal punishment, and at the apparent prudery and hypocrisy of the laws governing sexual behaviour. Such Muslims strongly argue that many punishments in the name of Islam are simply the cultural consequences of rulers and governments who flout the true spirit of Islam, and twist its values. They say that, in the modern age, Shar'iah needs to be reformulated to reflect a civilised society.

This offers little consolation to many who remain baffled by what they see as the barbaric practices taking place in the name of Islam every day. It is difficult for someone in Paris, New York, or London to understand that some of their counterparts in the Muslim world remain able to divorce themselves from the administration of local justice. Even as they are discussing astrophysics or international finance, they are aware, yet uncomplaining, that down the road an errant wife is being stoned to death, a petty thief is having a hand cut off, or for some lesser offence someone is being flogged in the market square. If this were only a relic of the cruelty of Muhammad's own era, the West might consider it reprehensible. However, many consider that even worse than the execution of such tough justice is the explanation given for it: that it is being done in the name of God.

Though the West is quick to condemn the brutality, some Muslims claim that it is in no position to judge. Advocates of Shari'ah argue that, before attacking Islam's penal system, we should remember the violence and injustices perpetrated by the West against many Muslims. We should also remember that only a century and a half ago rebellious soldiers or sailors were flogged publicly, and sometimes died. Flogging occurred even in British schools sixty years ago. Admiral Nelson hanged from the yard arm his dinner guests against whom his country had a grievance. After the Indian Mutiny, the victorious British army burnt the villages they passed through before executing the mutineers by strapping them before the open barrel of a cannon. Such examples of brutality would now be condemned as war crimes. Only a little earlier, men and women were burnt alive for holding proscribed Christian beliefs, or those that defied Christianity.

Before being shocked, it is important to understand what is really going on behind the sensational headlines. When defending Shari'ah, Muslims argue that non-Muslims often fail to understand that the difference between our systems of punishment is one of evolution, rather than an example of an inherent brutality. They say that, when chatting to their family and neighbours about Islamic justice, non-Muslims condemn it without having understood life in the society that it governs. Some insist that our penal system is too lenient and too liberal: it not only fails to ensure that God's will is respected, but it also leaves His people vulnerable in this world. They maintain that Shar'iah law provides a proper, structured, and fair system before any extreme verdict is given. To people used to the lengthy trials of, say, a murderer, in common law, in which lesser courts first have to agree that there is a case to be answered, before a trial takes place in a higher court, the often fast official justice in many Islamic countries comes as a shock.

Supporters of the Shari'ah system insist that due regard is paid by their courts to extenuating evidence, just as it is in common-law courts. The mental state of the accused, and other relevant details that would be presented by the defence at the Old Bailey would just as surely be heard by the Shari'ah judges. Extreme penalties are awarded only in exceptional circumstances and when there is no alternative, they say; and there are different degrees of punishment. *Jinayah* penalties cover cases of murder and bodily harm, and are issued according to 'an eye for an eye' or *diyah* – payment of blood money to compensate the victim's family. The Qur'an states, 'The reward for an injury is an equal injury back; but if someone forgives instead and is reconciled, that will earn reward from Allah.' *Ta'zir* penalties, such as fines and community service, are the least severe.

The most controversial sentences – flogging, amputation, the death penalty – are allocated under what is known as *hadd*. Judges are advised to adopt caution and avoid such sentences wherever possible. 'Avert the infliction of the *hadd* penalties on Muslims as much as you can, and if there is any way out, let the person go – for it is better for a ruler to make a mistake in forgiving than make a mistake in punishing (Tirmidhi).' The *hadd* penalties cover the most serious crimes – alcohol (*sukr*), theft (*hirabah*) including armed robbery, arson, assassination, kidnapping and hijacking, slander (*qadhf*), adultery (*zinah*), and apostasy (*riddah*). Muslims in favour of Shari'ah insist that minutely detailed rules govern the administration of any of the severe punishments awarded for each of these crimes, and that they are only issued as a last resort.

Flogging, the commonest, and therefore the most criticised, of punishments, is carried out under controlled conditions, observing a long list of rules that limit the amount of injury that can be inflicted. Strict rules prevent any damage to the head, face or genitalia. In any flogging women, must be fully clothed, and must not be flogged on very hot or very cold days. The purpose of the flogging is only to bruise the skin and superficial tissue. The arm of the flogger must always be held against his side, and this ensured by tucking a copy of the Qur'an under the arm. Should the flogger's arm be raised over his shoulder, the Qur'an would fall, and the transgression of the rules become obvious. The list of rules is long: there are many others. But whether these rules are all obeyed in an age in which torture and cruelty is commonplace in jails is sometimes questioned. Although no lasting damage is done, and compared with nineteenth-century European floggings the beating is relatively mild, the sheer number of strokes administered produces almost intolerable pain.

However well regulated, a sentence of flogging for the mere consumption of alcohol causes extreme consternation amongst the significant non-Muslim drinking masses. Drinking alcohol in moderation is thought of as a reasonable way to relax and unwind after a busy day. It astounds us that this seemingly harmless daily habit would warrant a flogging in some other part of the civilised world. Some Muslims point out that alcohol in strict Islamic countries has assumed an importance that it did not have in the days of the Prophet Muhammad. On this subject, Muhammad took a more lenient line than would now be advocated in Saudi Arabia: the Prophet did not advocate the seeking out of drinkers in their own houses away from public. The determining factor as to whether drinking was acceptable, one that is still the case in many

Muslim societies, was whether the drinking led to public disorder. The law regarding alcohol as it now enforced in some Muslim countries is the law of the land, rather than that laid down in the Qur'an. There were no objections to flogging those who were drunken and disorderly in public.

If the beatings ordered by Islamic courts can shock non-Muslims, amputation of the hand for theft appalls them. Muslims, for their part, are staggered that theft and burglary have become such a widespread part of everyday life in the West. They often find Christian condemnation of amputation hypocritical and quote the New Testament, reminding us that it was Jesus who said, 'If your hand causes you to sin, cut it off. It is better for you to enter life maimed than with two hands to go to Hell.' Perhaps the way we might best come to understand the serious penalties for theft in Islamic states such as Saudi Arabia, Iran, and Syria, is that robbery is still thought of as a serious crime against individuals and against the neighbourhood. It is the West that has changed its attitude to theft. In Muslim countries, thieves bring shame and disgrace on their family and all who are associated with them. A pious Muslim is appalled by even the thought of theft, let alone the act, because of the dishonour to his or her family, and the disapproval of God. Owing to the seriousness of the charge, advocates of Shari'ah argue that the case against an alleged thief is carefully explored, and any witnesses are interviewed. A first-time offender is unlikely to be sentenced to amputation: it is normally reserved for the recidivist who refuses to change his ways.

Amputation is not the most drastic punishment administered in the Muslim world. Capital punishment still exists in many Islamic states, just as in many Christian countries. There are several types of offence that are so heinous in the eyes of Islam that they merit the death penalty. Although murder is not strictly speaking a *hadd* crime under Islamic law, Muslims and non-Muslims are unanimous when discussing penalties for murder. In both instances, it is a question of the Old Testament rule of a life for a life, as well as an eye for an eye and a tooth for a tooth. Murder in Islamic countries simply is punishable by death, a fact that is accepted both by the criminals and the judiciary.

Any person who has had a close and beloved relative murdered might arguably be within their moral, if not their legal, rights to take revenge. British law has always fiercely condemned the kind of summary justice in which a person takes the law into his or her own hands. Shari'ah law, like European or American law, has no respect for the concept of revenge killings either, even though in some remote areas blood feuds between families have continued for generations. But should a murderer be found guilty, the murdered person's family is given the opportunity to forgive. Money is often exacted as an outward sign of the murderer's guilt and repentance – although the thought that anyone's grief at the death of loved one could be lessened by cash is abhorrent to many people.

Muslims who interpret the Qur'an to mean that it sanctions revenge killings, blood killings, and honour killings are now mainly people who have been brought up in tribal communities. It is not a concept supported by most Muslims. To suggest that the justification for these revenge killings is entirely cultural, however, ignores the most obvious interpretation of the Qur'an, which says:

'The law of equality is allowed for you in cases of murder (*surah* 2:178)', and 'Do not take life, except for just cause. If anyone is wrongfully killed We give his heir the right to demand retribution or to forgive; but let him not exceed bounds in the matter of taking life (*surah* 17.33).' The essential teaching of the Qur'an, that of an eye for an eye, a tooth for a tooth, is the Old Testament biblical opinion, which altered only with Jesus Christ's 'Turn the other cheek', in the New Testament. Even after that, in Christian countries revenge, although not approved, tended to be ignored for centuries by the authorities. This attitude persisted in Italy or Northern Ireland until recently, though there are few countries in which Christianity is taken more seriously.

There are few aspects of Islamic law that are more incomprehensible to most non-Muslims than the Islamic approach to adultery. Most non-Muslims regard the stoning or hanging of an adulterous woman or man to be one of the cruellest and most alarming aspects of Islamic law. It runs contrary to the sanctity-of-life principle that most non-Muslims hold dear. No suburban Lothario would expect his girlfriend to be stoned to death or hung from a crane if he was found *in flagrante delicto* with her. The penalty would seem totally out of proportion with the crime itself. In the secular West, the preservation of a woman's virginity if she is unmarried, or her faithfulness if she is, though they might well be respected, do not have the same implications of honour as they do in Islam.

Many surveys show that a majority of male adults, and a sizeable proportion of women, have committed adultery. Their revulsion at the draconian Islamic penalty may perhaps be inspired by a sense of 'there but for the grace of God go I.' However, there is also a feeling that a sin, even if it is a sin of the flesh that some faiths would consider grievous, is in a different league from crimes such as murder, bodily harm, or rape. If someone is to be punished for these lesser sins, it should be by judgement in the life hereafter rather than in a courtroom. While non-Muslims regard fidelity as a question of personal morality, strict Muslims argue that the reverence for marriage in Islam makes a woman's immodesty and lack of self-control worthy of the extreme punishment. A woman's honour in a Muslim country has a position unequalled in non-Muslim social and family life. To destroy it is to destroy the fabric of someone else's family, and to befoul them in the face of God, their family, and their friends. It is a most appalling crime, a theft that deprives the whole family of their dignity before God and man.

The Prophet Muhammad had some experience of the shame that a mere accusation of adultery could bring on the accused and their family. His wife was accused of adultery, and as a result Muhammad received a revelation in which God told him that capital punishment was only appropriate when the evidence was irrefutable; and that it applied only to committed, married, and free Muslim citizens. People accused of the sin of adultery should not be condemned unless the act had been seen by at least four witnesses. There was a hazard to those who bore false witness, or who could not substantiate their claims. In the common-law courts of the West there is often some sympathy for a woman who falsely claims that she has been assaulted, and there is discussion of the psychological reasons for this. But in Islamic countries, an accusation made without proof is punishable by flogging. Not surprisingly, few cases of adultery came before the courts in the Prophet's lifetime, and that is the case today. In his lifetime, the occasional case in which someone confessed to adultery so that he could meet his Maker without blemish was recorded, and is still quoted 1,400 years later. Those cases of adultery that today make the headlines are mainly cases in which a woman has knowingly been living with an unmarried man as his wife. Nowadays, DNA evidence is accepted in lieu of the four eye-witnesses, but the availability of such technology is limited in some parts of the Islamic world, so it remains the case that it is unsurprisingly very difficult to assemble sufficient evidence to guarantee a conviction.

Blasphemy is also an extremely grievous crime under Shari'ah law. Muhammad's own response to such attacks was to hold firm and be patient, hating the evil but not the person who had succumbed to it. This, however, was not the reaction of many Muslims in response to the Danish cartoons that appeared in 2005 when a *fatwa* was issued and death threats made against those responsible. So, what was it that caused such offence? Images of Muhammad wearing a bomb as a turban, or on a cloud refusing entry to the martyred *Mujahaddin* because he had run out of virgins, angered Muslims because they linked the Prophet directly with terrorism. Similarly, Salman Rushdie's novel in which a Muslim attacks the Prophet Muhammad was deemed a more serious offence than attempting to undermine or refute the teachings of Islam. If a non-Muslim attacks the faith, rather than the Prophet, it would not be acceptable nor forgiven, but it would not warrant such a severe sentence. If someone offends God, that is a matter between them and God. But if someone who has had the advantages of being born and raised as a Muslim attacks Islam, it could be construed as an attack on Islam that would endanger the brotherhood. It could then deserve the death penalty. but it would be preferred if they recanted and repented.

Apostasy, known in Islam as *irtidad* or *ridda*, meaning 'turning back' is the sin of renouncing Islam. If someone who has been raised as a Muslim betrays their upbringing and rejects the brotherhood of Islam, they thereby undermine the unity of the faith, endangering those within it. To be born a Muslim is a privilege. To fail to recognise this, and to renounce the advantages that God has given you, is an insult to God, a subversive action that may hazard the brotherhood, a heinous crime. It is accepted that proselytising is commendable, but the Qur'an lays down that it should be within bounds. Allah said, 'Let there be no compulsion in religion (*surah* 2.25)', but this has not stopped Muslim armies making life uncomfortable, or even extinguishing life, if people did not, readily and rapidly, find that they wished to join Islam.

The Qur'an does not specifically allocate the death penalty to the sin of apostasy, although its condemnation of such people who commit it could not be stronger: 'The curse of Allah, the angels, and all humanity is upon them. They shall remain under it forever; neither will their punishment be lightened nor will they be given respite. But for those who repent after this and mend their ways, then truly Allah is indeed forgiving, merciful.' The death penalty is normally only given if the sinner has committed murder or treason. Even then, it is allocated in the most extreme circumstances and by the most orthodox regimes.

It is hard for non–Muslims to understand how an attack on God is considered a lesser offence than the denigration of the Islamic faith and those who uphold it. But those who attack God's teachings are undermining the efforts of others to follow His way, and in doing so they erode the structure of Islamic faith and culture. They have totally failed to appreciate the importance that the Islamic faith places on the necessity of leading a good life in this world in order to gain access to the next. They are thwarting God's will, a far more grievous offence than being rude to an omnipotent deity.

The biggest deterrent for a Muslim is not the fear of brutal punishments under Shari'ah, but that all sins are recorded and will be accounted for on the Day of Judgement. Human judgements are fallible, but at then no one will be able to escape the law of God. He alone is the perfect judge, and it will be He who dispenses justice. The Muslim's consolation is that God is always merciful and understands human frailty. As He told Muhammad, 'My mercy prevails over my wrath (*Hadith* Qudsi).' In everyday life, if someone has a well-developed conscience he or she will know God's will, and will follow it. Only God can provide real forgiveness, and it is therefore the moral obligation of all Muslims to make good any wrongs that they have inflicted on others. This may be scant consolation for a non–believer rotting in a damp subter-ranean cell, but for those who do believe, it may give them the courage and determination to keep going.

CHAPTER 24

Unity or division?

Even those whose only knowledge of Islam is derived from television and radio are least aware that one of the criticisms made against Muslims is the desire to establish a global caliphate. Bearing in mind the concerns that many people have about Shar'iah law, the notion that the United Kingdom and other countries in the West could one day be ruled by that law strikes horror into the hearts of many non-Muslims. The fear is that a European expansion might begin from those parts of the United Kingdom in which there already is a predominantly Muslim population. Tensions remain high between Muslim and non-Muslim; and what many people are asking is, first, what exactly Muslims are aiming to achieve in the modern age, and, second, how likely it is to happen.

It is widely known that Muslims, whatever part of the world they come from, are united with deep sense of oneness, or *ummah*, with other Muslims, and empathise passionately when they perceive their brothers to be wronged. The brotherhood is so strong that the image of a human body is used as a metaphor to describe it. If it loses limbs or organs, its very existence may be destroyed. This bond carries with it a sense of egalitarianism which is further demonstrated by the fact that in most Muslim countries neither priests nor princes are bowed to. At the mosque, men pray side by side, regardless of their origins or social status. All men are equal in the eyes of God, and no automatic rights are granted to one man over another – even by virtue of being a Muslim. There is no organised church in Islam, no priestly caste (in contrast, for example, with Christianity). *Imams* and Qur'anic scholars are respected, but not revered. God is one and man is one, and this is reflected in mankind's spiritual oneness: the Qur'an tells Muslims that God created us from a single soul. 'Believers are one single brotherhood, so make peace and reconciliation between two contenders, and revere Allah, that you may receive mercy.'

Muhammad was known to be deeply against the sectarianism or divisions that existed between his own followers and companions in Medina. He opposed anyone who caused enmity or upset, and is quoted as having once said, 'All mankind belongs to one human family'; also that 'Believers are like parts of a building, each part supports the others.' After the Prophet's death, the goal of spreading the message of Islam so as to create a single, unified state powered early Islamic conquests, in which the Islamic drive for unity saw incursions from Asia into the Balkans, and as far to the West as Spain and North Africa.

The concept of a world united by Islam is a dream held dear by the majority of Muslims. Such a united state of Islam, known as *khilafah,* they say, might be geographical, or equally pan-geographic – that is, a single rule over all

Muslims regardless of nationality or race. It would be ruled by a caliph, elected via an electoral process named *bay'ah* or 'mandate', and sworn in on the Qur'an and *sunnah*. Such a person would be of impeccable character and would command the respect of all Muslims. Many Muslims would like a descendant of the Prophet to take up this role, of whom they maintain there are many today (including the current Queen). Such a person would seek to unify all Muslims, and would govern a territory and people that would become known as the Dar-al-Islam, the land of Islam. Devout Muslims would see this land as being subject exclusively to the rules and constraints of Shari'ah law. They argue that the common law used in secular countries at the moment allows practices that contravene the basic principles of Islam: adultery, homosexuality, gambling, prostitution. Others recognise that some aspects of Shari'ah are cruel, and would accept a single state of Islam without the need for Shari'ah law.

Most Muslims accept both scenarios as being an ideal, rather than a likely, outcome in the years to come. The cracks and schisms in Muhammad's legacy that appeared so soon after the Prophet's death grew deep in the early centuries of Islam, and have failed to resolve themselves ever since. Principally, the divide between Sunni and Shi'a Islam has dominated the political, cultural, and religious life of Muslims ever since the seventh century. Today the family of Islam is still, in reality, an extremely fragmented one, and scholars nowadays refer constantly to what they call the pluralism of Islam. However, whilst there are a number of different branches of Islam, the overwhelming majority of Muslims – around nine in every ten – are

Sunnis. Traditionally, Syria, northern Iraq, Saudi Arabia, Egypt, the United Arab Emirates, and Oman have been entirely Sunni. Turkey, North Africa, Asia, Albania, and parts of the former Yugoslavia, notably Bosnia, are Sunni-dominated. The Shi'a minority has always been centred on Iran, Eastern and Southern Iraq and South Asia. But even though some areas of the Islamic world may be predominantly either Sunni or Shi'a, it is not correct to say that 'Arab' can be equated with being Sunni and 'Iranian' with Shi'a. Many recent conflicts in the Middle East, including the Iraq-Iran war and the invasion of Kuwait, occurred in areas where the balance between Sunni and Shi'a is more evenly matched. This has, to some extent, disguised the international predominance of the Sunnis.

Shi'as are further subdivided into different groups, that include the Ithna'Ahari (or 'Twelvers'), the Isma'ilis, and Zaydis. For 1,400 years, the descendants of the original Shi'as have continued to campaign for leadership by the direct descendants of Ali. Shi'as argue that their path is directly based on the teachings of Muhammad, whereas, they claim, Sunni Islam is no more than the result of the deliberations and machinations of the scholars of the ninth and tenth centuries, who came to power as the caliphs of the Empire after the Prophet died. Sunnis, of course, reject this claim, insisting that their Islam is the 'true' faith. Broadly speaking, the difference between Sunni and Shi'a Islam is considerably less than that between Roman Catholicism and low-Church Christianity.

The pious often assume their lifestyle and beliefs to be superior to those of the people around them, but no group has pursued the importance of unification throughout the world with such ardour as some sectarian Muslim groups. Such extremist Muslims exhibit attitudes that are unacceptable to non-Muslims, whilst similarly disapproving of moderate Muslims. Groups such as Hizb ut-Tahrir and its offshoot the Muhajirun regard the instigation of *kilafah* in the world as paramount. Without it in place, Islam is incomplete and unsatisfactory. Quoting as the basis for their conviction a *hadith* that predicts *kilafah* will come back to the world, they insist the caliphate it should be realised at any cost to themselves, even the surrender of their own lives. The Muhajirun was officially disbanded in 2004, but new extremist groups have sprung up with similar ideologies. Al-Ghurabaa (derived from the word *gharaba* meaning to 'depart', 'withdraw' or 'be absent') is a group widely believed to include many of those from the disbanded Muhajirun. They often quote a *hadith* that says, 'Paradise is for *al-Ghurabaa* – the strangers.' Their rationale is that since the *ummah* of Islam has failed, they have been selected by God to follow the true Islam.

The Saved Set is another group who believe they are the true followers of Islam, on the basis of a *hadith* by Tirmidhi, in which Muhammad tells of the seventy-two sects of Israel, stating that his *ummah* will be fragmented into seventy-three sects, all of which will be in hell-fire except one chosen one. When asked which one, the Prophet replied, 'It is the one to which I and my companions belong.' This idea of being special, the chosen ones, has encouraged members of such groups to lay down their lives in what they see as the glory of martyrdom in the name and service of God. Rather than spreading the word of Islam by force, some have resorted to militant expansionism to make their point. They condemn moderate Muslims, arguing that they are not proper Muslims and are *kuffar* (infidels) if they do not agree with their point of view. They accuse them of being asleep, lazy, and unwilling to make the ultimate sacrifice for their God.

Many moderate Muslims, however, are angered and frustrated by such groups and their opinions. The idea that they alone understand the true meaning of Islam is regarded as *takfir*, or bigoted. Such people, moderates say, spoil the entire reputation of Islam with their narrow interpretation of the faith – a stance that further infuriates the extremists, who argue that they are being side-lined and patronised. Such deep division within the ranks of Islam seems to fly directly in the face Muhammad's efforts all those centuries ago to unite people from all faiths under one single constitution.

In the modern world, the rift between non-Muslim and Muslim has become ever deeper. For the most part, the enthusiasm that moderate Muslims show for unification is a reflection of the egalitarianism with which they view all of humanity. The desire to spread Islam is thus rooted not in militant expansionism, but in a desire to share the love of God with all of mankind. Shakespeare wrote that 'One touch of nature makes the whole world kin,' but it will require more than a touch of anything to resolve the conflict within the brotherhood of Islam, and there will have to be a philosophical, religious, and cultural revolution before the non-Muslim world is converted.

Chapter 25

Love is the answer

The schisms within Islam are not reflected simply in the rift between Sunni and Shi'a, or between different schools such as Wahhabism and Hanbalism, or even by extreme and moderate interpretations of the faith. An important – and very different – movement within the family of Islam is Sufism, sometimes known as *tasawwuf*, or the mystical branch of Islam.

In the centuries following the Prophet Muhammad's death, Sufism first began to flourish in response to the intellectualism and dry legalism of the Islam jurists and theologians. Not just male but female Sufis became known and respected. They mixed freely with men, and found their own voices. In the thirteenth century, often deemed the golden age of Sufism, the renowned Sufi poet Jalal ud-Din Rumi taught that the acceptance of God's will was the ultimate attainment and that the way to achieve this was through the abandonment of any personal ambition or material wealth. Submitting oneself to God in this way constituted the highest form of love. This asceticism is thought by some to be reflected in the origins of the word

Sufi, a term derived from the Arabic *suf*, meaning 'wool', which might refer to the sparse woollen robe that goes with a simple lifestyle. Other scholars, however, say that the term might have its root in the Greek *sophos*, meaning 'wisdom', or even *safa*, meaning 'purity'; still others say it might be derived from *safwe*, meaning 'the chosen ones'.

Since then, and through most of Islamic history men have been both scholars and Sufis. Both formal and spiritual knowledge have been regarded as two separate yet intrinsically linked sides of a well-rounded Muslim. It is a classic development in the life of a Muslim scholar to realise, as al-Ghazzali famously did, or indeed Muhammad Abduh, that being a master of formal knowledge fell short. Formal knowledge of the Islamic scriptures had to be given depth with spiritual insight. Although there has been a criticism of the extravagant practices of some Sufis through time, as represented by Ibn Taymiyya, it has only been from the relatively time of al-Wahhab that Sufism itself has suffered major opposition within the ranks of Islam. Indeed, many of the leaders of Islamic reform over the past two hundred years or so have actually been Sufis themselves – of a modest nature.

In the modern age Sufism itself has sometimes received a bad press amongst the more orthodox branches of Islam. The ultra traditionalists have argued that Sufism deviated from the true path of Islam. Although Sufi teachings did not and still do not allow alcohol or drugs, other Muslims regarded with horror the Sufi use of chanting and dancing, and even alcohol and drugs in some countries, in an effort to induce transcendental experiences. Orthodox Muslims have regarded the (often flimsy) association of Sufism with astrology, numerology, and alchemy as dabbling with forces beyond human understanding. Although most Sufis do not dabble in magic, some bizarre methods of worship have existed, open to abuse by charlatans. Claims by some Sufis that they had managed to achieve union with the Divine were severely frowned upon by orthodox Muslims, who saw Sufism as a self-centred path, rather than one that focuses on others. They also saw the notion of complete obedience to a *shaykh* as unwise.

Medieval Sufi poets such as Hafiz and Sadi have also received opposition from the stricter branches of Islam. Perhaps some of this is unsurprising, since such poets wrote of God in openly erotic language, telling of the ecstasy experienced in achieving oneness with the Divine. In his work, Gul'istan described the emotional experience derived from dancing as being the zenith of the feelings of which a human being is capable. 'But how render, with the language of man, that which is beyond human powers? The words that we use cannot express other than what is common to our material and gross ideas. He who enjoys ecstasy and returns again to his ordinary state, does not retain any idea of it, because he has become man, whilst previously Divine love had consumed in him all that belonged to human nature.'

As some Sufis have come under increasing pressure to abandon their teachings, they have been persecuted and driven underground in some Islamic countries. In the West, however, Sufis can now practise openly without fear of reprisals. Many belong to one of two main orders, the Naqshbandis, whose members are Sunni Muslims and follow the Turkish Shayk Nasim, fortieth in line from Abu

Bakr. Other Sufis belong to the Murabitun order, and follow the Scottish Shaykh Abd-al Qadir. Centres of Sufism are known as *zawiyahs* or *kanqahs* in Iran, *tekkes* in Turkey, or *ribats* in Africa.

Sufis champion the idea that sacrifice of the self is key to serving God. By following an inner, spiritual journey a person can purify the soul and achieve oneness with God. Sufis argue that the true spirit of Islam is love. Above all else – knowledge, justice, freedom or greatness – love is paramount. All Sufis teach that oneness with God is achieved by loving Him and other people. The same principle is given voice in the Christian commandments to love God (the first and greatest commandment) and to love one's neighbour as oneself. While in this world, Sufis are devoted to the study of the truth, and are pre-eminently concerned with displaying their adoration of God, an adoration that exemplifies the extent of their desire to experience unity with Him. They believe that the power and mercy of the Creator is revealed in all His creatures. The Qur'an says: 'All mankind is of, and will return to, Him,' and this is the Sufis' doctrine.

The Sufi's journey towards understanding is known as the *tariqah*, meaning 'way' or 'path'. A student is known as a *murid,* a disciple who owes allegiance to a single master, or *shaykh*. It is a system of teacher and pupil that goes back to the Prophet Muhammad and his companions. There are varying stages, or columns, through which people pass before they reach the ultimate goal of oneness with God, but few achieve this. Novices need a teacher to guide them through the difficulties they will experience as they seek their goal. As well as being a teacher, the *shaykh* is also a shield against evil thoughts and temptations. Grade by grade, disciples advance, mastering all the mystical states, from honesty, *sidq*, and self-analysis, *muhasaba*, to spiritual ecstasy, *sukr*, the love of God, *mahabba,* and understanding, *ma-rifa*. Finally, they reach the fourth degree, which leads to God. They now see Him in all things.

Sufis believe that the Prophet himself was a Sufi and, as such, believed in the importance of the mystical elements of Islam. In support of their contention they are prepared to quote from a great many different *hadith*s. They also declare that the Caliph 'Ali, one of the two claimants to the role of successor to Muhammad, was well versed in their beliefs. Hassan and Hussain, two of the sons of the Caliph 'Ali, together with two other respected holy men, Kumail ibn-Zaid and Hassan al-Basri, strove to continue the traditions of the Prophet according to this emphasis on an inner spiritual path of Islam.

Some, but by no means all, Sufis become dervishes. Dervishes are entirely devoted to their search for the truth, as well as being engaged in the adoration of Allah, a union they desire with all the ardour of divine love. They believe the Creator is diffused through all his creatures; He exists everywhere and in everything in the known universe. They compare the emanations of His divine essence to the rays of the sun, and it is re-absorption into the divine essence to which they aspire. They believe that the soul of man is not from God but of God. Some maintain that God has entered or descended into the devout, that the Divine Spirit enters into all those who are of a truly pious and intelligent mind. Some believe that God is as one with every enlightened mind, and that the immortal part forms its union with God and becomes God. Others hold that God is in all things and that everything is God.

All dervishes aspire to the true spirit of asceticism, renouncing the pleasures of this world. Provided that he could achieve some degree of oneness with God, Sufis say that a dervish would even be prepared to give up hope of benefiting from the pleasures of Paradise, gaining his satisfaction from the sense that he was submitting to the will of God through devout contemplation of God's beauty. A dervish hopes that the Paradise to which he goes will be inhabited, not by those seeking the pleasures of *houris*, but by the pious, the holy, and the prophets.

Sufis who become dervishes have always been required to abandon worldly comforts, and to seek the awakening of the heart through submission, and dancing. Music is the food of the soul, and the soul's love is expressed through sound and movement. The dance, and the music of the flute, which is favoured by dervishes, represent the harmony that exists between these and the rest of God's creation. As the dervishes whirl, as they dance for joy, they utter lamentations interspersed with sighs, signifying their yearning to be at one with God. Their ardent desire to be united to him allows them to detach themselves from all unworthy passions. Mevlevi dervishes are not alone in using what is called the *daur*, or 'rotating dance'.

It is said that Jalal ud-Din Rumi, when he founded the Mevlevi dervishes in Turkey, became in the habit of rising from his seat and whirling around and that this was the start of the commonly-used term 'whirling dervish'. Rumi's extraordinary spiritual powers and their supernatural nature were said to arise from his ability to transcend the material world by spinning. It is written that if this spinning had not been accompanied by music, he would have become so locked in some mystical union that he would have disappeared from his devoted companions on earth. The choice of music stimulated his spirit, yet kept his feet on the ground. For the Mevlevi dervishes, the music that accompanied prayer varied between that of the mystical flutes, instruments made from natural canes or reeds, which made soft and gentle music reminiscent of many aspects of nature. Although gentle, the music had the power to excite the senses, so that those taking part could achieve a state of rapture and holy inspiration that would help them achieve oneness with God.

There are several orders of Sufi dervishes, including the Qadiris, the Khalwatis, the Bairamiand, and the Gulshanis, all of whom have practised this dance for centuries. Some remove their turbans as they entwine arms with their brethren in the dance. They lean their shoulders against each other, gradually raising their voices with each turn as they repeat the chant, '*Ya Allah*' or '*Ya Hu!*'. And while some dervishes chant as a means to achieving oneness with Allah, others use arm movements to reflect the light of heaven on to the ground - like the beating wings of a beautiful butterfly.

Another order, the Rifia, is much more controversial. The Rifia make use not just of dancing but also fire in their devotions. It is said that they can become so carried away by religious ecstasy, known as *halat*, that it is claimed they can withstand contact with red-hot irons or stabbing with sharp instruments. Dervishes transported by frenzy have been known to lick the red-hot poker, bite it, or hold it between their teeth, and even to cool it as it rests in their mouth. If there is any pain, they bear it without complaint. Within minutes of completing their devotions, known as *zikr*, the presiding *shaykh* would walk around the hall and breathe upon the wounds. After sometimes rubbing in some of his saliva, he would say prayers over them. Within twenty-four hours, if there had previously been any evidence of injury or wounds, they had healed and no mark was to be seen.

Such strange practices continue to strike suspicion and disapproval into the hearts of many mainstream Muslims who argue that Sufism is not the true form of Islam. And many Sufis themselves dismiss stories of the bizarre in the name of their branch of Islam as scaremongering. Sufism today nevertheless continues to have a major influence within the wider Islamic family. All genuine Sufis hold dear the key values of Islam as a peaceful, compassionate, and loving religion. For them, Islam is emotional, intuitive, and informal. Its association in more recent times with anything other than peace, they say, is the very opposite of the true spirit of Islam.

CHAPTER 26

The struggle of Jihad

The message of love and tolerance embodied by Sufism is in direct opposition to the perceived association of Islam with violence, an association at the heart of a clash of cultures that threatens to engulf the world in a third great war. With the nuclear capabilities of Middle Eastern states as well as Western ones, the threat of large-scale devastation seems very real indeed. But would such a war be a holy war? Are the terrorist acts perpetrated by al-Qaeda and its associates the consequence solely of political statements made by those aggrieved by what they see as the injustices inflicted on all Muslims? Is Islam, on any level, responsible for the outrages? Or is Islam itself being twisted out of context, as many argue?

Over the past twenty years, the word *jihad* has become as much a part of the English language as 'blitz', and it represents a return to close combat as the rule rather than the exception. Suicide bombers who walk into a bar or restaurant, or join the end of a bus queue, before their bomb explodes, can look in the eye the people they are about to kill. One thing especially surprising to many non-Muslims is the cult of the female *jihadi*. Although most suicide bombers are male, recently more women have become fighters, although traditionally Islamic women do not take up arms. For male martyrs, there is a well-established belief that there will be 72 virgins waiting for them in Paradise (though this number varies, depending on whom you speak to), but what is there for the female martyr? Some Islamic scholars suggest that in heaven a female martyr becomes Queen of the Virgins, and rules over them.

Women are increasingly inspired by the same political ideals that drive their radical male counterparts. In some cases, the driving factor may be as much one of personal revenge for the death of someone they have loved as it is for the cause. With the increasing emancipation of women in Muslim countries comes activism that would previously have been unheard of. Hanardi Jaradat, a 29-year-old Palestinian lawyer from Jenin, blew herself up on 4 October 2003, killing twenty-one other people, including women and children, at Maxim's, a restaurant in Haifa. In her suicide tape, she stated that she was happy to be avenging her brother's death. Was this the case? Or did extremist groups take advantage of this woman's grief to mould her into a killer? Non-Muslims argue that many of the women drawn into the extremist cause have had difficult backgrounds, and have often been abused or neglected while growing up. Muslims disagree, many finding the suggestion offensive that a Palestinian woman has been brainwashed, neglected, abused or opressed by her own men to commit a terrorist act. They argue that women have equal rights under Islam. If Hanardi watched her brother die and decided to act in accordance with the eye for an eye Islamic law by seeking revenge on those occupying her land just as Israelis kill freely her people, she is acting of her own will, which is justified according to Islamic law. They cannot see how there is one rule for Western non-Muslim women to join the army and fight and another for Muslim women who are simply branded as a terrorist who has been abused and neglected by her own people.

Jihad, argue Muslims, is not just another word for terrorism, as some non-Muslims might assume, but a complex concept that has been at the heart of the Muslim faith since its inception. The word is not found anywhere in the Qur'an itself, but it does appear in the teachings and traditions of the Prophet Muhammad recorded after his death. *Jihad*, one aspect of which is to wage holy war in defence of Islam, is considered an obligation of faith, and is sometimes referred to as the sixth pillar of Islam.

Within the Islamic world debate continues about the true nature of *jihad*. The word itself is derived from the Arabic root *j-h-d*, meaning 'effort' or 'striving'. In Arabic texts, this has became increasingly synonymous with the narrower sense of struggle and fighting, but one original rendering was 'striving in the path of God'. By and large, scholars agree that *jihad* refers to the effort to practise religion in the face of oppression or persecution: this could be fighting the evil in one's own heart, or standing up to a dictator. It does not refer exclusively to fighting a holy war; indeed, this is a disingenuous interpretation that has been perpetuated in part owing to some fundamentalists misusing the term themselves. Some Muslims limit the concept of defensive *jihad*, so that it applies only to situations in which a Muslim state has been invaded, such as in Palestine, for example. Others interpret the term 'defensive *jihad*' much more broadly; and the more radical deny that there is any distinction between internal and external, also known as the greater and the lesser, *jihad*.

It is impossible to understand the debate about *jihad*, and the emotion it generates, without first understanding the significance of *jihad* in the history of Islam. *Jihad* is as old as the religion itself. The division between the lesser and the greater *jihad* existed from the moment the concept became part of Islamic life. When a group of Muslims returned from a military raid, they were met by the Prophet Muhammad. He told them that although they had come back from their battle, this was only 'lesser *jihad*'. They still faced the 'greater *jihad*': the battle every man fights in his own heart against his baser nature. Muhammad's teaching was that people had to wage a *jihad* of the tongue by spreading the Islamic message, and from time to time they needed to use physical means to spread Islam – the *jihad* of the hand. By these means, justice would prevail.

Extremist Muslims interpret *jihad* solely in terms of holy war. They maintain that this is the only acceptable definition of the term, and that *jihad* has been used in this manner since the days of the Crusades. Suicide bombers may consider their interpretation no different from that of the Saracens in defence of Jerusalem. They are simply defending Islam. Moderates hold that the primary objective of *jihad* is to fight against oppression, without causing mayhem and misery. They say that using religion to support violence in the name of freedom and justice is the very opposite of what is meant by *jihad*. Meanwhile, non-Muslims claim that this debate shows how the Muslim world is fraught with double standards and ambiguities within.

Jihad as a means of ridding the world of non-Muslims has caused much controversy. The Qur'an gives guidance on this debate. God does not sanction the killing of those who refuse to accept the Islamic faith; rather, those who believe are told to 'bear with patience what they say, and when they leave give a courteous farewell'. 'Deal gently with disbelievers; give them enough time,' says another verse – the assumption being that they will see for themselves, without being coerced, that Islam is a way to a fulfilling existence in this life, and reward in the next.

Muslims agree that the *ummah* may, in self-defence, resort to military *jihad*. But the revelations of the Qur'an clearly specify the rules that govern waging a holy war. Such a war may only be declared in the name of Allah to restore peace and ensure freedom from tyranny. Islam does not permit holy war as a means of spreading the Islamic faith: 'Let there be no compulsion in religion,' the Qur'an says. Forced conversions would not be sincere.

Detailed rules of holy war are laid down in the Islamic scriptures. Islam stipulates that it is legal to wage war against four types of enemies: infidels, apostates, rebels, and bandits. Only the first two of these wars count as *jihad*. Fighting against ordinary criminals, rebels or bandits is not to be honoured with this title. Muslims also differentiate between offensive and defensive war. Only in a defensive war is *jihad* an obligation that falls upon the whole Muslim community. Muslims are commanded never to begin hostilities of any kind, not to embark on any act of aggression, not to violate the rights of others, and not to harm the innocent. Even hurting or destroying animals or trees is forbidden. War must be waged only to defend the religious community against oppression and persecution. The Qur'an stipulates, 'Let there be no hostility, except to those who practise oppression.' Therefore, if non-Muslims are peaceful, or indifferent, toward Islam, there is no justification for declaring war on them. The Qur'an allows for an eye for an eye, as the Bible does, but insists that the most virtuous path is forgiveness. After all, it is only for Allah to judge who has been wronged, and who has acted wrongly; and each will receive what they deserve in the hereafter.

The rules also dictate that in command of the troops there should be a leader who performs the double role of military commander and spiritual guide. A leader who was corrupted by power, or who became too dictatorial, could be executed if he refused, when challenged, to resign his position. The ancient rules also insist that the leader must not be motivated by desire for personal gain or glory, but only by the determination that the enemies of Allah should lay down their arms. Women, children, the old, and sick are under no circumstances to be harmed; and trees and crops must not be unnecessarily damaged. It is a precept that has been ignored by many of today's suicide bombers who argue that in any war there will be casualties. People will sacrifice their lives for their faith and their country.

It is well known that anyone killed in the name of *jihad* is a martyr or, in Arabic, *shahid*, or martyr, itself derived from the ancient Greek *martys*, which means 'witness', just as the Arabic term *shahid* also means 'witness'. The reward for martyrdom in *jihad* is eternal bliss in the afterlife. *Shahid* has been adopted by extremists to refer to those prepared to die because their love of Allah is greater than their love of self. By dying in His cause, they bear the highest form of witness to God.

It is hard to comprehend how such apparently high, noble ideals can be used in direct conjunction with the appalling atrocities witnessed by the world in recent years, but to explore how this can have occurred it is firstly necessary to examine the vital role in history of orthodoxy and politics.

CHAPTER 27

The rise of extremism

Politics and religion have been inextricably linked in Islam ever since the Prophet Muhammad became a political as well as a spiritual leader in Medina. Radical political Islam, however, is a relatively recent phenomenon. Until the middle of the last century it had been a relatively small movement, but when Abu'l Ala Maududi, a revered Islamic leader and philosopher, founded his Jama'at-e Islami party in India in 1941, he effectively laid the foundations of today's anti-Western doctrines, planting the seeds for Muslim condemnation of the secular world for its immoral behaviour and unsavoury influences. According to Maududi, *jihad* was a political and military struggle rather than an inner one, and Islam was at its heart a political ideology. It was an interpretation of the faith that was in turn to be picked up and expanded by a number of influential Muslim thinkers.

In Egypt, political Islam flourished further under the banner of the Muslim Brotherhood, or Ikhwan al-Muslimun, a movement originally founded by Hassan Al-Banna'in in 1928 to promote core Islamic values of piety and charity. But the movement quickly became radicalised. Al-Banna's writings, with substantial success, persuaded the public that Egypt had become dependent on the corrupt, secular West. Over time, the Brotherhood went on to become the biggest Sunni reform group in the twentieth century, and proved a powerful force against Western secular influences in the Middle East. Political Islam then journeyed to new extremes under the guidance of the Egyptian Sayyid Qutb, who maintained that all Muslim society had lost sight of what Islam really meant, citing modern man's obliviousness – or *jahiliyyah* – of its true revelation.

Qutb's own bitter experiences of torture and imprisonment at the hands of President Gamal Abdel Nasser had a deep effect on him. As a result, he concluded that the infidels who had carried out the brutality, plus every Muslim who tacitly went along with Nasser's regime, were to be condemned without mercy. Qutb now openly advocated the killing of infidels, wherever they lived in the world, and encouraged a war upon all Western influences. His works were to inspire future radical political groups such as Islamic Jihad, al Shabab and Tafkir wa'l Hijrah. Fundamentalists such as the Muslim Brotherhood were so fervent in their beliefs that they were prepared to defend their faith up to the point of death. In Iran, Ayatollah Khomeini caused public opinion to swing further against the perceived amorality of the West, as millions of Muslims became indoctrinated against what became known as the *gharbzadigi*, or so-called 'westoxification' of the world.

Another factor in the equation had been fundamentalism. Since the mid-nineteenth century, Islamic conservatives had been promoting Salafism, a purist, orthodox movement of Islam held the belief that all the ills of society derived solely from what they saw as non-Muslim corrupt secular practices. The *salaf-al-salih* (the righteous or pious predecessors), or the *sahaba* ('companions'), the *Tabi'un* ('followers') and the *Tabi' al-Tabi'in*) ('followers of the followers'), believed that only the companions of the Prophet and two succeeding generations were closest to and therefore were able to represent the true path of Islam. They cited a *hadith* by Bukhari: 'The best people are those of my generation, and then those who will come after them, and then those who will come after them.'

Pioneers of this movement were intellectuals at al-Azhar University in Cairo (although some modern Salafis now seek to distance themselves from such figures). These clever early interpreters included Muhammad al-Din Afghani (1839-1897), Muhammad Rashid Rida (1865-1935) and Muhammad Abduh (1849-1905). All three adhered to the works of early scholars such as Ahmad ibn Hanbal (d.855) and Taqi ad-Din Ibn Taymiyyah (d.1328) and Ibn al-Qayyim (d.1350). Al-Afghani was a political activist who had personally witnessed British colonial rule in India and campaigned against the discrimination of Muslims there and against the British invasion in Afghanistan. Al-Afghani's step forward, under the influence of Guizot's lectures on civilisation, was to see Islam as a civilisation. His concern was to find ways to make the Islamic tradition shine against the challenges of the West. Abduh, meanwhile, sought gradual social and legal, rather than political, reform. Their ideas were to have widespread influence – not only upon Egypt's nationalism, but as far as the Islamic revolution in Iran.

It was not only in Egypt and Iran that the perceived depravity of the West was denounced. Devout Muslims all over the world recognised the failings of secular society. In Saudi Arabia Muhammad ibn Abdul Wahhab (1703-92), a very pious, orthodox Muslim, had began the movement known as Wahhabism to erase what he regarded as the impurities and corruption he felt had crept into Islam. These included even other branches of the faith, such as Shi'ism and in particular, Sufism. Scholars seeking new interpretations of the faith or intellectualising it were branded as arrogant and in Wahhab's eyes, agents of the devil. According to his thinking and those who have since followed him even the term Wahhabism was regarded as derogatory. Instead, Wahhabi clerics preferred to be known as Salafis or traditionalists – conservatives seeking to adhere to the essential, pure values of the Qur'an.

In the early twentieth century Abdul-Aziz ibn Saud laid the foundations of modern Saudi Arabia. Since then, Salafi fundamentalism has flourished thanks to the discovery of rich supplies of oil in the desertlands, seen by its followers as a divine gift that has allowed their way of Islam to spread across the world. Muslims point out that this has been continually sanctioned, aided and abetted by America and the West. Wahhabism has also expanded its remit, along with revival movements in the 1970s and 1980s often referred to as Islamism. The movements are not to be confused. Modern Salafis do not like to be tagged with the Wahhabi label because they say Muhammad ibn Abd al-Wahhab did not found a new school of thought, but rather revived the pure, unadulterated Islam practised by the earliest generations of Muslims.

This dynamic spread of Islamic orthodoxy has inevitably been responsible for the growing intensity of anti- Western feeling. Salafis, in particular, reject not only Western ideologies as socialism and capitalism, but also Western concepts such as economics, constitutions and revolution. They regard politics itself as a Western activity, avoiding engaging it even with 'an Islamic slant'.

In addition to the expansion of orthodoxy and anti-Western ideas, recent decades have seen a series of critical events that have fanned further the fire of anti-Western feeling amongst many Muslims. Many Arab nations came to feel they had been sidelined on the global stage, and made to feel like second-class world citizens. This tendency reached its zenith at the end of the First World War, after the Turkish and German Empires were defeated and the then conquering powers divided up the Middle East, setting out artificial boundaries that rewarded those leaders who had done most for the victorious allies. Israel's conquest of Jerusalem and the Palestinian territories, the race riots in Malaysia in 1969, Pakistan's invasion of its eastern territory resulting in the creation of Bangladesh in 1971, the revolution in Iran, the subjugation of Kashmir, and Israel's invasion of the Lebanon in 1982 were world crises that had a gradual, cumulative effect on Muslim attitudes towards the West. All of these brought a sense of helplessness and disillusion amongst those who blamed Western governments for their failure to act as an ally.

Of all the troubles that stemmed from this, and the diplomatic double-dealing that was associated with it, those that involved the fate of Palestine have proved the most lasting and most contentious. The PLO has never accepted the Israeli occupation of what was once Palestine. They fought to regain independence, and unashamedly used terrorist methods in pursuit of this goal. They eschewed political attempts to solve the Palestinian camp problem in the Lebanon because they realised the strength of the political message that their presence there conveyed around the world. Hezbollah, the strict Shi'a Muslim organisation set up in the early 1980s, came to prominence after the end of the Lebanese civil war, and in response to the Israeli occupation of Lebanon. Hezbollah also adopted terrorism as a means of furthering its cause. The motivation of HAMAS and the PLO in their fight for a Palestinian state has much in common with that which inspired the IRA for seventy years.

As with the IRA, religion, politics, and the battle for territory were intermingled. However, crucially, HAMAS and Hezbollah are not generally regarded as terrorist groups by Muslims. In their eyes they are representing those who are simply oppressed and fighting a just war to free themselves from an enemy invading their land. They use suicide tactics only because they feel they have no other means to fight their enemy due to its powerful military capabilities. Just as in Iraq and Iran, they are acting under the eye for an eye Islamic law because they feel the power of NATO airstrikes and tank bombardment is a force they cannot stand up to. Therefore a guerilla strategy must be used to fight back.

The West took little interest in the savage war between Iraq and Iran, though they tended to support Iraq rather than Iran. The damage done to both sides in the course of the war was breathtaking, but, perhaps more significant was the tremendous impact on Sunni-Shi'a relations. It was probably the most significant event in the history of that enmity since the seventh century. Saddam Hussein, encouraged by the support he had against Iran, decided to fulfil a long-held ambition to acquire the small, oil-rich country of Kuwait. Despite Western warnings, he invaded it. The turmoil in the Middle East that followed this invasion, and the intervention of the Western forces, has increased the tensions in the Middle East and stimulated its different loyalties.

Events in Bosnia and Afghanistan in recent decades have also had a profound effect on the dramatic increase of extremism. It could be argued that the most severe arena for modern political Islam was the 1992-93 conflict in Bosnia. At that time Bosnia replaced Afghanistan as the new Islamic battleground, and many Muslims, including white British Muslims, lost their lives. It was Bosnia that brought extreme Islamic political motivation to the attention of the West. Many Muslims were appalled and angered by the British Government's refusal to help the Muslims against the Serbs.

Just a few years earlier in 1989, thousands of volunteers joined the *jihad* to drive the Russians out of Afghanistan in order to prove they were 'real' Muslims before God, and drive out the Communists. A war developed between Pushtun and non-Pushtun for control of Kabul, which the Pushtun, the *Mujahaddin* and the Taliban (with Pakistani army support) won. In the *Mujahaddin*, a rift developed between Osama bin Laden and the man who had been his mentor, Azam. Bin Laden had a heroic reputation among Muslims for his role in the struggle against the Soviets. He was charismatic, and said to be gentle and wise. But he grew more and more radical towards the West, and his views hardened with the Gulf War. After the Soviet defeat, Bin Laden went back to Saudi Arabia, but became *persona non grata* after his offer to help the Saudis deal with Saddam Hussein was rejected. He then set up a base in the Sudan, increasingly coming to see the world in view of Islam versus the West. His activities in the Sudan led him to feel that he would be safer back on the north-west frontier, and it was to that region he that he returned around 1996 and from which he began to systematically organise his military campaign against the West. Subsequently, more and more Western Muslims went to the camps he set up to train as *jihadis*.

By 1995, stories of atrocities carried out in the name of Islam were galvanising the Muslim political arena and the West. For many British Muslims what was most disturbing was that the victims of the massacres were white – what would happen if the same persecution happened here, and with Asians and non-whites? Extremist groups in Britain turned Bosnia into a highly political event, and circulated videos of the conflict. Moderate Muslims argued that Muslims should stick to the 'united body of Muslims', and avoid individual groups setting up camps. They maintained those camps were simply educational arenas in which to radicalise more Muslims.

The events of 9/11 in the United States changed the political landscape for Muslims everywhere, forever. Some became targets for reprisals. Many say that it was only then that they came to know what it was really like to be a Muslim. Many ordinary Muslims feel their religion has been hijacked by politics and terrorism; many say that extreme political Muslims use the name of Islam wrongly. Some feel they are being forced to bear a collective guilt, and that they are being asked to prove their allegiance to their country, whereas all they ever wanted was to be integrated into that society. At the same time many of those Muslims argue that 9/11 was not the single most audacious terrorist act in history compared to those of Hiroshima, Vietnam, black slavery or the unjustified war on Iraq that killed so many and which resulted in over ten years of sanctions.

Over the past decade, complaints about a range of global and domestic issues have fanned the flames of fury amongst Muslims wherever they live, and some cite the Islamic duty to defend Islam when it is under siege in order to justify the use of warfare and violence against the world at large. Many Muslims are dismayed by what they see as the double standards of Western governments. They want government policies to change, and feel more conscious than ever of their membership of the global Muslim family, and of their political identity. The recent invasions into Iraq and Afghanistan have fuelled the rage of radicalised Muslims everywhere. Their grievances do not just originate from extremist preaching, nor any precedents in the Qur'an, but a response to foreign policies created by Western leaders.

Muslims have been angered not only at the military heavy-handedness and the loss of life of their brothers and sisters in other countries, but at the intrusion into their cultural and religious freedoms. Young Muslim children are brought up hearing about all the injustices inflicted on Muslims in different countries at different times. Their parents rail at the arrogance of Western governments who believe they can act as the world's soldiers. They denounce what they see as the hypocrisy of the West, asserting that it appears to uphold values of democracy and freedom, but in reality it does the opposite. They argue that the war on terror is simply an excuse for gaining control of the copious oil reserves of the Middle East, and believe that there is even a conspiracy among those governments to develop Muslim lands to the advantage of the West. Above all, they are outraged at the abuses of human rights in Guantanamo and Abu Ghraib, and at the new British anti-terror laws that allow Muslims to be locked up without charge for days, or weeks. Why is there one set of rules for the West and another set for everyone else?

Whatever historians may decide about the effect of modern history on East–West relations, it remains the fact that millions of European Muslims consider that America and Britain have been utterly unjust in interfering with Iraq and Afghanistan. Although intervention may be deemed to have succeeded in Bosnia and Libya, the West has still much to answer for, Muslims say. In their opinion, the American–British axis has ignored the plight of those Muslims living in Palestine, while practically persecuting those living elsewhere. The Jewish lobby in America has guaranteed lasting protection for Israel, and that has created an unfair and destabilising effect in the region. Right or wrong, these opinions, and the resulting anger and frustration, are shared by many British Muslims.

CHAPTER 28

Unspeakable acts

Although many Muslims do not like to see the division of their community into 'radical' and 'moderate', there are some who do nevertheless hold extreme views. Radical Muslims today see the world in black-and-white terms. On the one hand there is the land of Islam, and on the other, that of the infidels. War is to be waged against anyone who disagrees. Terrorist campaigns by certain militant Islamic political groups have become a global phenomenon. Extremist groups draw upon the unrest and anger that exist in many parts of the Muslim world, and use the basic Islamic concept of *jihad* in order to make their political statements. A series of attacks on embassies and consulates in different cities have put militant Islam centre-stage. Thousands of lives have been lost, not only those of Americans and British citizens, but people from many parts of the world and of all faiths – all in the name of the religion of Islam. Such radical Muslims responsible for the atrocities regard themselves as an international force that can no longer be overlooked or contained. They say God is on their side. How can this ever be justified?

When the al Qa'eda terrorist network masterminded
9/11, in Western eyes the single most audacious terrorist
act in history, it changed the political landscape for
Muslims everywhere forever. This extraordinary boldness
heralded a brand new age in terrorism in which young,
disaffected Muslims – even in developing countries –
began to daydream about the immortality to be claimed
by dying for the Islamic cause. United by the disastrous
phrase the 'war on terror', disparate factions of extreme
Islam believed they now had an excuse to launch a holy
war against the West. They maintained that the violence
was justified by the actions of their enemies. They insisted
that their rage was not personal, but reflected the outrage
that all Muslims must feel for the assault on their brothers
or sisters in countries that had been 'interfered' with by the
West. They viewed the struggle in global and spiritual
terms, between values – truth and lies, good and evil. They
regarded killing themselves and murdering innocents as
military piety. Suicide in Islam is a mortal sin, and, rather
than carrying with it the promise of eternal bliss, earns the
one who commits it everlasting damnation. There is a
difference between facing almost certain death at the
hands of the opposing enemy, and killing oneself. One
leads to heaven, the other to hell. Suicide is *haram*, yet the
death of a martyr is, to the extremists, an honourable death
that any mother of a martyred child can take pride in.

To this date, no terrorist organisation has had the
global vision or capability of Al Qa'eda, which continues
to enlist Muslims from all over the world to wage a *jihad*
against the West. Al Qa'eda members are encouraged in
the belief that this holy war will have Allah's support,

because they are attempting to extend their own morality to displace what they see as the degenerate behaviour of the West. They are furious at the wars in Iraq and in Afghanistan, and at human rights abuses permitted and even perpetrated by the coalition forces.

Terror in the name of Islam is being perpetrated in our modern, civilised society and no difference of faith is now seen as sufficient to justify the cruelty and carnage brought about in the name of the religion. Yet Muslims stress that Islam does not encourage or allow terrorism. They maintain that terrorism is a political word used by corrupt leaders to influence hatred towards Muslims when they decide to intervene in a foreign territory. They remind us that acts of violence have not just been committed against the West or Westerners. Within Islam sectarian acts have continued to terrify and horrify Muslims all over the world, perpetrated by those within the faith adopting a narrow interpretation of its ideology.

Contemporary Salafist literalists are very different from that of its twentieth century pioneers, Abdu, Rida and al-Afghani. In recent times Salafism has given rise not only to the severe oppression of women in those states where it is exists, but to a raft of bloody acts. Salafism is meant to be non-violent and, indeed, there are many Salafis who are peaceful. There are, however, many Salafi scholars who oppose vehemently the present-day occurrences of jihad involving acts of terrorism against innocents. They say that no individuals have the right to take the law into their own hands whatever the circumstances. Even the closes of the Prophet's companion's never killed a single opponent, even when faced with invectives during his first thirteen years at Mecca. Nor did they kill anyone in retaliation when the Prophet was pelted with stones at Ta'if.

Still, many people argue that ever since Muhammad ibn Saud of the house of Saud in Saudi Arabia signed an agreement in 1744 with Abdul Wahhab there have been indiscriminate murder and violence by those who adhere to extreme, orthodox forms of Islam. In the twenty-first century, Salafism has become linked directly to Al Qaeda and other extremist groups who advocate the killing of innocent civilians in the name of Islam, whether they are non-Muslims or simply Muslims who do not share their own particular view of Islam.

Today, 'Salafi jihadism' is a phrase coined by scholar Gilles Kepel. It refers to a specific school of Muslims who actively support *jihad* in the form of terrorist violence specifically in order to realize their political objectives. Salafi jihadists actively seek to practise their ultra-violent methology by means of indscriminate attacks and suicide bombings, wherever and whenever the opportunity arises. Although such people constitute a tiny proportion of all the world's Muslims (journalist Bruce Livesey estimates the ration at one per cent), nevertheless these individuals pose a significant danger to the world as a whole. Egyptian scholar Tawfik Hamid says that it is oil wealth has led to the expansion of this regressive and violent Islam begun in the late 1970s. Like all Salafis, the Salafi jihadists believe that both their view of Islam and their acts of violence are supported by God. They say this truth has been manifested in Saudi Arabia's wealth. Aided by a United States of America keen to exploit the natural resources of the deserts and Saudi riches, the ideology adopted by such extreme Muslims has thus spread throughout the globe. It has not only resulted in the loss of innocent human life, but in the systematic destruction of places of historical interest and Muslim heritage in and around Mecca because of accusations of idolatry and polytheism.

When Islam is labelled as synonymous with terrorism moderate Muslims not only remind us of the extreme factions within their religion. They also point out that we would do well to remember that terrorism as a weapon in political conflict has, of course, many precedents in history that are nothing to do with Islam and that at no time in history has religion truly been the only cause of conflict. British, Spanish, Dutch, and Portuguese imperialism were each rooted in the threefold concerns of territorial gain, the acquisition of riches, and the spread of religion. There was state terrorism under Nazi Germany and Soviet Russia, but it is really revolutionary movements that have exerted the real power and expertise of terrorists. Since Tiberius and Caligula, via Robespierre during the French Revolution of 1789, and through to the IRA, history is peppered with examples. Catholics empowered by the Spanish Inquisition were ruthless in pursuing what they regarded as religious impurity, and had no hesitation in imprisoning, torturing, and, if necessary, killing the impious. Reliance on terror was such a prominent feature of the French Revolution that the period afterwards from 1793-94, during which the politics they embraced had become dominant, was known as the Reign of Terror.

In Great Britain Vikings murdered St Edmund because he would not renounce his Christianity. Crusaders left England and France in the hope of spreading Christianity in the Eastern Mediterranean, and recapturing Jerusalem. In the nineteenth century, violence, including physical and mental torture, assassination, kidnapping and brutality, was a feature of political and religious evolution in Europe and America. The Ku Klux Klan was started as a terrorist organisation after the American Civil War in 1861 by people in the south of the United States who had fought with the Confederate army, and could not bear to be aligned with the Yankee north. In Europe, terrorism has been perpetuated by the IRA in Ireland and the British mainland, by the many revolutionary parties that attempted to overthrow the Russian monarchy, and by those who turned the Balkans into a cauldron of conflict for 150 years. The First World War was started by a terrorist act, when Archduke Ferdinand was murdered in Sarajevo in 1914. Even Queen Victoria suffered an assassination attempt.

The modern concept of terrorism in the name of Islam has acquired subtleties of meaning and connotations far beyond not just its history, but its dictionary definition. Islamic extremists now use terrorism as a strategic device in making war while attracting attention to a cause to make political points. When waging war against an enemy, terrorists today make no distinction between soldiers and civilians. By killing and maiming innocent men, women and children, and laying waste their homes and businesses, at the same time destroying the services that hold together a district, they inflict psychological as well as physical damage on their opponents. As the incidents have been more murderous and destructive, they have attracted more publicity. One supporter of the Palestinian cause has been quoted as saying: 'The world is talking about us now. When we hijack a plane, it is worth more than a hundred soldiers killed in battle.'

Just as globalisation has inevitably increased multi-cultural tension and discord, so has the speed with which news can be relayed and reactions to it expressed. The internet has enabled extreme Islamic groups to quickly become established in every corner of the world. The questions raised by the terrorist acts are no longer discussed only in the newsrooms and university common rooms, but also in mosques and *madrasas*. Facts and guesses, opinions and arguments, anger and agreement, are rapidly churned around the globe, and are accessible equally to those who are concerned by them and to those who couldn't care less. Modern communications make the actions of militant Islamists centre-stage, whether the incident has happened in London, New York, Madrid or Bali.

Everyone is aware that there are conflicting beliefs within Islam, but the day of the New York bombings showed how complex the reality is. Those Muslim suicide-bombers who carry out such atrocities are celebrated amongst their supporters, and deemed to be martyrs. Although the direct response of many moderate Muslims reflected the same horror, shock and anger as the rest of the world, reaction to the attacks in the Muslim media varied. Some Muslims, particularly those in the Middle East, were considerably less appalled, as television pictures of their street parties showed.

After 7/7, the British public was astounded, and deeply concerned, by polls that showed a sizeable minority of British Muslims understood the motivation of the terrorist bombers. A poll for Channel 4 discovered that nearly a quarter of those asked thought that the bombings were justified; one in ten understood why British Muslims might want to carry out a suicide bombing in Britain; and one in five respected Osama bin Laden. The British Sufi Council found that between seven and nine per cent of Muslims in this country thought that suicide bombing was justified, and that any loss of life was an acceptable sacrifice. Muslims spoke then of a covenant of security, an unwritten treaty to which they all felt honour-bound. Any attack on innocent people or harm to an Islamic country was regarded as an attack on all Muslims. Extremists such as Abu Muhammad and Mohammad Siddique Khan were retaliating for injustices that all Muslims understood.

Such findings were disturbing to non-Muslims living in Britain. It was the first time suicide bombers had attacked on the home shore. Even more unsettling, the bombers were born in Britain. Some British Muslims became targets for reprisals, and many ordinary Muslims felt that extreme political Muslims were using the name of Islam wrongly and that the Prophet Muhammad would never have condoned violence in this way; that to twist Islam to justify their cause was unforgivable. For some Muslims even to elide extremism, Islam, and terrorism in the same speech has been offensive. Many Muslims who are not particularly religious, and are certainly not sympathetic to fundamentalist ideology, have condemned outright any act of violence in the name of Islam. They felt insulted that by the suggestion that, simply because of their backgrounds, faith and dress, they have been viewed with suspicion, arguing that it was not terrorism or extremism that was being targeted, but Islam itself.

Despite this fact, some anti-Muslim scholars at the time argued that the extent to which moderate Muslims could legitimately distance themselves from extreme acts in the name of Islam was debatable. Patrick Sookhdeo, the Director of the Institute for the Study of Islam and Christianity, in an article in *The Spectator* entitled *The Myth of Moderate Islam*, wrote, 'By far the majority of Muslims today live their lives without recourse to violence, for [the Qur'an] is like a pick-and-mix selection. If you want peace, you can find peaceable verses. If you want war, you can find bellicose verses.' Sookhdeo went on to explain the principle of so-called Qur'anic abrogation, whereby verses revealed to Muhammad in his later life over-rode those revealed to him earlier. 'The peaceable passages in the Qur'an,' he wrote in the article, 'are the early ones, dating from Muhammad's time in Mecca.' After the flight to Medina in 622, the revelations became decidedly 'more belligerent, with the result that the mantra 'Islam is peace' is almost 1,400 years out of date.' Unsurprisingly, it was a controversial view that stirred deep unrest amongst the ranks of all Muslims.

In the twenty-first century, the duty to defend Islam when under attack may to most people seem to be no more than an excuse for terrorism. Indeed ultra-orthodox Muslim groups believe the conflict will end only when all accept God's law and accept a global caliphate. The rest of us – moderate Muslims included – hope a compromise of some kind can be achieved, believing as we do in 'live and let live' as opposed to 'an eye for an eye'. After many outrages, battles and injustices, peace may well be achieved eventually. In the mean time, people will have to reconcile themselves to the fact that the process will possibly extend over many more generations to come. Some hope may be gleaned from the Qur'an itself, which states, 'Goodness and evil cannot be equal. Repay evil with what is better. Then he who was your enemy will become your intimate friend.' Physical fighting is permitted only until the enemy seeks peace, then it must stop. 'If they seek peace, then you seek peace. And trust in God – for He is the One that hears and knows all things.'

CHAPTER 29

Is peaceful co-existence achievable?

As the number of Muslims living in the West has grown, so has the sense of division between us, not least because of the events and threats that continue to take place in the name of Islam. Remembrance Day poppies burnt by radical organisations such as Muslims Against Crusades only serve to inflame public feeling and to incense ordinary peace-loving people on both sides. With the passage of time, probably measured in generations rather than decades, better integration might well eventually take place, but it would be unrealistic to expect it to occur rapidly. The current rift between Muslim and non-Muslim extends to almost every aspect of everyday life, the outward and visible signs of Islam reaching beyond the veil, even beyond the everyday practice of medicine, law, and education. Although Muslims hold dear many of the same things as non-Muslims – from decent moral values, charity towards others, to looking after our families as well as our planet – they also honour different mores, not only in the law courts but in the doctor's surgery, schools, and in operating theatres.

To many non-Muslims, who have no way of understanding what their Muslim neighbours are thinking, the
only indication of how well those neighbours are
integrating is how they dress and behave in public. Basic
questions are therefore being asked. Can those who are
first-, second-, or, in some cases, third-generation Western
Muslims be loyal to their faith *and* to their country? Will
they ever agree that their duty is to maintain the national
constitution of the country in which they live, and that
their primary concern must be for the welfare of their
fellow citizens? Will they obey the common law that has
evolved over the past thousand years, or will they insist that
the law of their faith should determine justice?

Recently Muslims have demanded, and been given the
right in some supermarkets, not to have to serve customers
who are buying alcohol, although since then other
moderate Muslims have suggested that handling a bottle of
whisky would not be as disturbing to most Muslims as
selling bacon, pork, or potted shrimps. In response, many
people feel that, by failing to acquiesce with traditional
local and national customs in medicine and education,
their Muslim neighbours are rejecting both the idea of
integration and the hand of friendship that was held out to
them when they first came to this country. Some feel hurt,
even enraged, by this apparent lack of appreciation of the
local way of life. They are haunted by the fear that those
who have been in their country only for a generation or
two are intending, in time, to take it over. No better
example of the failure of Muslims and non-Muslims to
become a cohesive unit is the inability and reluctance of
some Muslims to learn to speak the native language. This

is not helped by the teaching in mosques and Islamic schools, in Shari'ah meetings and on Muslim radio stations, of Arabic or other Islamic languages as the first language. It is a potent argument for multi-faith schools.

Since the suicide bombings by Islamic extremists, it is inevitable that proportionally more Muslims than non-Muslims are now subject to police interference. But unfortunately every time any Muslim is stopped and searched, his neighbourhood sees it as an example of racial and religious harassment. Laws that make it an offence to glorify terrorism – the raiding of Islamic bookshops for extremist literature; and radio stations searched by Special Branch – are regarded as religious harassment by many Muslims, whereas non-Muslims understand these as wise precautions taken by a government that wants to prevent further terrorist outrages.

Various steps *are* being taken to combat radicalism. In Britain the Government has drawn up plans for anti-radical Muslim schools. Nevertheless, many teachers are concerned that in some existing Islamic classrooms young Muslims from the start of their schooling become aware that there are double standards. In Muslim classrooms, one-minute silences may be held for those who have lost their lives carrying out a bombing, whereas when they leave the classroom they go on to hear the incident being roundly condemned. The question remains: will it ever be possible for young Muslim children living in the West to learn Islam in such a way that they will be equally loyal to their country and their religion?

The chance of a reasoned, detached compromise that would lead to racial harmony is now being undermined by the fear that Muslims are part of an international community that is under siege. The more the members of the community feel this, the more their feeling of Islamophobia will extend, and non-Muslims will become increasingly hostile. This sentiment has been exacerbated by the fury many Muslims feel about the 'war on terror' launched by our leaders some years ago. In their minds it has turned those who they look to for support and understanding into an adversary.

Western governments believe that Muslims living in their societies will in future have to learn to separate their political opinions from their basic religious beliefs. Many Muslims believe that this is impossible, and that political life, like every other aspect of their life, is dominated by, and intrinsic to, their Islamic faith. They say the conflict between faith and patriotism is a fight for the mind. The question is: who is going to win?

CHAPTER 30

Islam and the future

Not only is there a fight for the mind. In the twenty-first century, Islam's greatest battle is one for the heart, as the world faces perhaps its greatest challenge since World War Two. Although the battle-lines of the new conflict of understanding between Islamic and non-Islamic peoples have not so much been drawn up, as have evolved, they cannot be ignored.

Before the Second World War there were no Muslim communities of any significance living in Britain, France, Holland, or Germany. Today, more Muslims live east of the Hindu Kush than to the west of it and Islam is easily the fastest growing religion in the West today. It is estimated that there are now between fifteen and twenty million Muslims living in Europe, and eight million in America. Analysts such as Omer Taspinar predict that the Muslim population of Europe will nearly double by 2015, while the non-Muslim population will shrink by three and a half per cent, owing to the higher Muslim birth rate. Another researcher, Esther Pan, predicts that, by 2050, one in five Europeans is likely to be Muslim. Professor Philip Jenkins of Penn State University estimates that, by 2100, Muslims will compose about twenty-five per cent of Europe's total population, although some authorities refute this figure as a wild guess. At the same time Muslims are acculturating (for better or worse) to European ways. Wonderful comediennes such as Shazia Mirza and Shappi Khorsandi, and the rock groupie Roxana Shirazi, have helped to change the way non-Muslims think about Muslims today.

As the controversy over Islam's reputation continues, it is difficult not to wonder what the Prophet Muhammad would have made of the direct association of his faith with the rise in terrorism, its treatment of women, and archaic system of punishment. How would he have reacted at finding the religion he once fought so hard to establish the object of fear and mistrust for millions?

The recent uprisings in the Middle East prove beyond doubt that young Muslims already have a very significant voice in world affairs, and as they are not afraid to make it heard their influence will surely become of increasing importance in world politics. It is hoped that this passion for political freedom and reform in the society in which Muslims live can also be directed towards reform of the Islamic cultural practices that others may find archaic and unacceptable. Muhammad himself is credited as being a champion of peace and co-operation among all human beings, whatever their race or faith. It was his belief that fragmentation leads to ignorance and weakness all round.

Issues related with religion in a hyped up climate of politics and constant media coverage are not easy to deal with. Given the current divisions between Muslim and non-Muslim and the popular stereotyped perception of

Muslims and Islam in the West, they may lead us to pessimisim and frustration. How we turn these raw emotions into opportunities is an important concern. Islam undoubtedly needs strong leaders to help resolve tensions in the generations to come. The spread of extremism, whether advocated by Islamic groups or non-Islamic organisations, requires strict control. Muslim leaders must persuade terrorists operating in the name of Islam that, however valid they believe their point to be, the killing and maiming of innocents is not the way to make that point. More steps need to be taken to disentangle Islamic economies in the Middle East from those in the West. More inter-faith discussion needs to take place, leading to agreement between Muslim and non-Muslims on central issues such as integration. Although many Western Muslims are highly educated, in some Islamic countries educational opportunities are limited. Since education is a key, perhaps funds from oil-rich nations could be employed to improve the quality of education of Muslims living in poorer Islamic countries. We need to work together to achieve trust, but this trust works both ways. Several Islamic centres of study already work to promote understanding of Islam in the West. Other initiatives, such as the Sakinah Campaign, are under way and reaching out to persuade extremists to modify their radical ideas. Yet many institutions in Muslim countries still actively preach hatred against the West. Teachers and preachers sometimes take advantage of young and impressionable Muslims to poison their minds against non-Muslim beliefs and practices. Work needs to be done to redress the balance.

In order to achieve peaceful co-existence, the political grievances also must be analysed. Accusations of arrogance and the allegations of hypocrisy of governments should be examined by those in power, cultivating a climate of modesty, a willingness to listen rather than act. The media can assist by striving to present any conflict between Islamic and non-Islamic groups factually, without bias. Islam should never be presented as being inherently evil, as many Muslims maintain the Western press is liable to do. If all this can be achieved, it might help to combat the Muslim sense that there is a conspiracy against Islam. In the interests of world peace, distortion for the sake of sensationalism will have to be brought to an end.

Tolerance and acceptance are required on all sides. It would be naive to think we can set aside our cultural and religious differences, and indeed counterproductive – since it is our diversity that gives us depth and makes our society rich. The Prophet Muhammad tried to establish a pluralistic society in his lifetime, but today Muslim society is anything but pluralistic. This poses a great challenge for all Muslims. As Muhammad himself taught, 'We need to practise that which is common between us.' Surely we must all seek to build upon shared interests and moral values, whilst retaining our identities and without compromising principles. Rumi wrote, 'We see the sunlight shining into many different courtyards. If we take away the walls, we will see it is all the same light.' Beneath cultural and religious difference we are people – bound together by our joys, sufferings and humanity. We must open our minds and hearts, and reach out in search, not of those things that draw us apart, but of those that connect us.

Glossary

adhan call to prayer
akhira afterlife
al-hujr al-aswad the black stone of the *ka'ba*
amal action
ansars the helpers of Medina
ashura 10th Muharram (death of Hussain)
asr mid-afternoon prayer
ayah Qur'an verse
ayat al-sayf the sword verse
ayatollah senior shi'ite imam
bida innovation
burka garment which fully covers a woman's body
chador covering sheet
dar al-Barzakh between life and death
dar al-Islam the land of Islam
din the faith, dedication of one''s life to Islam
du'a personal or private prayer
eid or *id* literally 'returning often', celebration of renewal
    in Islam
eid al-adha feast of sacrifice
eid al-fitr feast to end Ramadan
fard compulsory
fajr pre-sunrise prayer

fatiha opening prayer of the Qur'an

fatwa legal opinion or verdict

fiqh the study of Islamic law

ghayb the unseen universe

ghusal total washing of the body

hadd most serious crime under Islamic law

hadith saying of the prophet Muhammad

hafiz someone who knows the Qur'an off by heart

hajj pilgrimage

hajji or *hajja* honorary title given to one who has
    completed the pilgrimage to Mecca

halal allowed

haram forbidden

halat religious ecstasy (cf Sufism)

hijab head-covering veil

hirjah literally 'cutting off', Muhammad's flight from
    Mecca

houris ethereal women, inhabitants of paradise

ibadah literally 'servant', meaning worship

ihram pilgrim's clothes

ihsan realisation

ijma the consensus of legal views

ijtihad the working out of Islamic principles by reasoned
    thought

imam prayer leader

iman faith

iqamah the second call to prayer

irtidad literally 'turning back', apostasy

isha the night prayer

i'tikaf religious retreat

jahannam hell

jannam heaven

jihad striving or struggle to do God's will

jinn spirit beings

ka'ba shrine in Mecca

kalifah caliph or successor

kanqah Sufi teaching centre (Iran)

khamr intoxicating substance

khilafat the dominion of the successors of the Prophet
   as leaders of the Muslim community

khitan circumcision

khutbah sermon

kunya parent's name taken from child

kursi stand on which the Qur'an can be placed

kiswah the black cloth covering the Ka'ba

Kufic script style of Qur'an

kuffar infidels

lalyat al-bara'at the Night of Blessing (full moon before
   Ramadan)

lalyat al-isra wal miraj the Night of the Prophet
   Muhammad's ascent to heaven

lalyat al-Qadr the Night of Power

laylat al-Miraj the Night of Ascent

madhhab school of Islamic law

madrasah school for Islamic learning

maghrib the nightfall prayer

makruh disliked or disapproved of

Ma'il script style of Qur'an

mandub recommended

masjid mosque

mihrab niche indicating direction of Mecca

minaret mosque tower

minbar pulpit for sermon
mithaq binding agreement
mubah a matter of conscience
muezzin one who issues call to prayer
mujtahid Muslim jurist qualified to interpret scripture
mutah temporary marriage
nafs the 'lower self', one's human desires
Nashki script stye of Qur'an
niyyah intention
purdah seclusion of women
qadr predestination
qisas 'eye for eye' revenge
Qur'an the holy book of Islam
rakah unit of prayer movements
Ramadan the Islamic month of fasting
rawdah gathering to commemorate the dead
riba interest on loans
ridda apostasy
risalah prophecy
sadaqah charity
salah ritual prayer
salaam gesture of peace
salat al-Jumah Friday prayers
sawm fasting
shahadah bearing witness
Shari'ah the ethical and legal way of Islam
Shi'ite supporters of Ali
shirk the division of the oneness of God
subhah prayer beads
Sufi follower of Islamic mysticism
suhur dawn meal before fasting

sujud prostate prayer position
sunnah the example of the Prophet Muhammad
Sunni mainstream Islam
surah Qur'an chapter
taharah purity
takfir bigoted
tajweed the reading of the Qur'an
talaq divorce
taraweeh Ramadan prayers
tariqah literally 'the way' or 'the path', Sufi order
tasawwuf spiritual insight, used to refer to Sufism
tasbih prayer beads
taqwa being conscious of God
tawaf al-wada final prayers at the hajj pilgrimage
tawhid the oneness of God
tayammum ritual dry wash
teelawah reading with intent
tekke Sufi teaching centre (Turkey)
ulema religious scholars
ummah the brotherhood or family of Islam
umrah pilgrimage outside the hajj period
walimah wedding party
wudu ritual washing
wuquf the stand at Mount Arafat
zakah or *zakat* religious tax
zawiyah Sufi teaching centre
zinah sin, adultery
zuhr midday prayer

Bibliography

History

Atlas of the Islamic World since 1500, Frances Robinson, Oxford,1982

Cambridge History of Islam, Frances Robinson, Cambridge, 1996

The Oxford History of Islam, John Esposito, Oxford, 1999

Islam the Straight Path, John Esposito, Oxford, 1998

The Arabs in History, Bernard Lewis, Penguin, 1950

Islam and the Integration of Society, W. Montgomery Watt, London, 1961

The Majesty that was Islam, The Islamic World 660-1100, London, 1974

Religion and State in Iran, Hamid Algar, Berkeley, 1969

Arab Historians of the Crusades, Francesco Gabrieli (trans E J Costello), London, 1984

A History of the Arab Peoples, Albert Hourani, London, 1991

A History of Islamic Societies, Ira M Lapidus, Cambridge, 1998

A History of Medieval Islam, J. J. Saunders, London, 1965

The Jews of Islam, Bernard Lewis, London 1980

An Introduction to Shi'a Islam, Moojan Momen, London, 1985

What Every Christian Should Know about Islam, Raqaiyyah Waris Maqsood, Islamic Foundation, 2000

Hadith Literature, It's Origin, Development and Special Features, Muhammad Zubayr Siddiqui, Islamic Texts Society, 1993

The Muslim Discovery of Europe, Bernard Lewis, Phoenix, 2000

Islam in Modern History, Wilfred Cantwell Smith, London, 1957

Islam: A Social History, Karen Armstrong, Phoenix, 2000

The Muslim Creed: Its Genesis and Historical Development, A. J.

Wensinck, Cambridge, 1932

The Venture of Islam, Conscience and History in a World Civilization, Marshall G. S. Hodgson, London, 1974

Muslim Intellectual: The Struggle and Achievement of Al-Ghazzali, W. Montgomery Watt, London, 1948

A History of Muslim Philosophy, M. M. Sharif, Wiesbaden, 1963

The Qur'an

Heart of the Koran, Lee Hixon, Quest Books, 1988

Understanding the Qur'an, Themes and Style, M. A. S. Abdel Haleen, I. B. Tauris, 2010

The Meaning of the Holy Qur'an, Abdullah Yusuf Ali, Amana, 2004

Secrets of the Koran: Revealing Insight into Islam's Holy Book, Don Richardson, Hampton Roads, 2005

The Life of the Prophet

A Biography of the Prophet, Karen Armstrong, xx 1991

Muhammad and the Conquests of Islam, trans Virginia Luling and Rosamund Linell, xx, 1968

Muhammad, the Man of Allah, Sayyid Hossein Nasr, London, 1982

Mohammad, Maxine Rodinson (trans Anne Carter), London, 1971

Muhammad at Mecca, W. Montgomery Watt, Oxford, 1953

Muhammad at Medina, W. Montgomery Watt, Oxford, 1955

Muhammad's Mecca: History in the Qur'an, W. Montgomery Watt, Edinburgh, 1988

Muhammad and the Qur'an, Rafiq Zakaria, Penguin, 1991

Muhammad, His Life Based on the Earliest Sources, Martin Lings, Inner Traditions, 2006

Muhammad, The Man and His Faith, Tor Andrae (trans Theophil Menzel), HarperColllins,1977

Muhammad and the Conquests of Islam, Francesco Gabrieli (trans Virginia Luling and Rosamund Line), Weidenfeld, 1968

Tenets of Islam

The Hajj, The Muslim Pilgrimage to Mecca and the Holy Places, F. E. Peters, Princeton, 1994

Fasting in Islam, Ali Budak, The Light Inc, 2005

Muslim Devotions: A Study of Prayer Manuals in Common Use, Constance Padwick, Oneworld, 1996

Mysteries of Fasting, Ibn Al-Arabi, Kazi Inc, 2009

Reality of Prayer in Islam, Sadegh Angha, MTO, 1998

Jihad in Classical Medieval Islam, Rudolph Peters, Princeton, 1996

Consuming Habits: Drugs in History and Anthropology, edited by Jordan
Goodman, Paul E. Lovejoy and Andrew Sherrat, 1995

Ideals and Realities of Islam, Seyyid Hossain Nasr, ABC Int, 2001

Family and Culture in Islam

Family History in the Middle East: Household, Property and Gender,
Edited by Beshara Doumani, State of New York Press, 1999

A Guide to Parenting in Islam, Muhammad Abdul Bari, Ta-Ha, 2011

Debrett's Manners and Correct Form in the Middle East, Sir Donald
Hawley, Debrett's Peerage Ltd, 1984

The Camel and the Wheel, Richard W Bulliet, Harvard University
Press, 1975

Ottoman Traveller, Robert Dankoff, Eland, 2011

Kitab at-Tabikh, Muhammad ibn al-Baghdadi, ms Istanbul, 1226

Women in Islam

Women and Gender in Islam, Leila Ahmed, Yale University, 1992

Women and the Koran, Anwar Hekmat, Prometheus, 1997

Women and Islam: An Historical and Theological Enquiry, Fatima
Mernissi (trans Mary Jo Lakehead), Oxford, 1991

The Woman in a Muslim Society, Muhammad Sharif Chaudhry, Al
Matbaat-ul- Arabia, Lahore, 1995

The Hidden Face of Eve: Women in the Arab World, Nawal El Saddari,
Zed Books, 1980

Women and Sex, Nawal El Saddari, Zed Books, 1984

Status of Women in an Islamic Society, Bano Asfar, Anmol Pubs, New
Delhi, 2004

Women in Muslim Societies, edited by Herbert L. Bodman and
Nayereh Tahid, Lynne Rienner Publishers Inc, 1998

Islam, Gender and Social Change, Yvonne Yazbeck Haddad and John
Esposito (eds), Oxford, 1998

Islam in the Modern Age

The State We are In: Identity, Terror and the Law of Jihad, Hamza Yusuf
Hanson, et al, Amal Press, 2006

Radical Reform, Tariq Ramadan, OUP USA, 2009

Western Muslims and the Future of Islam, Tariq Ramadan, University
    of Oxford Press, 2005
The Muslim Mind, Chris Waddy, Grosvenor Books, 1991
The Crisis of Islam, Bernard Lewis, Phoenix, 2008
The Trouble with Islam Today, Irshad Manjij, St Martin's, 2005
The Islamist, Ed Hussain, Penguin, 2007
Only Half of Me: Being a Muslim in Britain, Rageh Omaar, Viking, 2006

Sufism
Sufism: An Account of the Mystics of Islam, A. J. Arberry, London, 1950
The Mystics of Islam, Reynold A. Nicholson, London, 1914
The Triumphant Sun: A Study of Mawlana Rumi's Life and Work, A. M.
    Schimmel, London, 1975
The Sufi Path of Love: The Spritual Teachings of Rumi, William C.
    Chittick, Albany, 1983
Islamic Spiriituality, Seyyid Hossein Nasr, London, 1987
Sufi Expression of the Mystic Quest, L. Bakhtiar, London, 1979

Fundamentalism
The Battle for God: Fundamentalism in Judaism, Christianity and Islam,
    Karen Armstrong, HarperCollins, London, 2001
Islamic Fundamentalism, Abdel Salam Sidhared and Anonshirivan
    Ehteshani (eds), Boulder, 1996
Islamic Fundamentalism, Youssef M. Choueiri, Continuum, 2010
The Prophet and Pharoah, Muslim Extremism in Egypt, Gilles Kepel
    (trans Jon Rothschild), Saqi Books, 1985
Jihad in Islam, Abud Ala Mawdudi, Lahore, 1976
The Vanguard of Islamic Revolution, Seyyed Vali Reza Nasr, California, 1994
Islam and Universal Peace, Sayyid Qutb, American Trust Pubs, 2006
Milestones, Sayyid Qutb, Islamic Book Service, 2006
Islam and Revolution, Sayeed Ruhollah Khomeini (trans Hamid Algar),
    Berkeley, 1981

Islam and the West
Orientalism: Western Conceptions of Orient, Edward Said, Penguin, 2003
The War for Muslim Minds: Islam and the West, Gilles Kepel, Harvard, 2006
The Emergence of the Modern Middle East, Albert Hourani, 1981
Islam and the West: The Making of an Image, Norman Daniel,
    Oneworld, 2009

Index